100 GROUP
(BOMBER SUPPORT)

RAF BOMBER COMMAND IN WORLD WAR II

Ghosts of the airfields. Author

100 GROUP
(BOMBER SUPPORT)

RAF BOMBER COMMAND IN WORLD WAR II

Martin W. Bowman

Pen & Sword
AVIATION

First published in Great Britain in 2006 by
PEN & SWORD AVIATION
An imprint of
Pen & Sword Books Ltd
47 Church Street
Barnsley
South Yorkshire
S70 2AS

ISBN 1 84415 418 1

A CIP catalogue record for this book is
available from the British Library

Printed and bound in Great Britain
By CPI UK

Pen & Sword Books Ltd incorporates the Imprints of Pen & Sword Aviation,
Pen & Sword Maritime, Pen & Sword Military, Wharncliffe Local history,
Pen & Sword Select, Pen & Sword Military Classics and Leo Cooper.

For a complete list of Pen & Sword titles please contact
PEN & SWORD BOOKS LIMITED
47 Church Street, Barnsley, South Yorkshire, S70 2AS, England
E-mail: enquiries@pen-and-sword.co.uk
Website: www.pen-and-sword.co.uk

CONTENTS

ACKNOWLEDGEMENTS

This is where I came in. Back in the late 1960s and early 1970s my friends and I would visit airfields in Norfolk, especially the more accessible ones immediately surrounding Norwich – and there are many – ostensibly to look for bits of wrecked aircraft. I soon tired of this, but my interest in aviation matters increased a hundredfold with the discovery, like some modern day Howard Carter (who once resided in Norfolk), of a multitude of artwork adorning the walls of the old barrack huts, Nissens and other buildings on the ex-RAF airfields and American bases. In 1971 this interest prompted me to compile books on the units stationed at every airfield in the region and *Fields of Little America* was first published in 1977. I could not foresee that I would be retracing these same steps twenty-five years later! A Kodak Instamatic was not the best means of capturing the paintings, cartoons and pin-ups, but in the late sixties it was all I had and buying film was not cheap for a teenager. After all, the artwork would still be there for a few years would it not? It had survived the ravages of time for almost thirty years so it seemed reasonable that a return trip could always be made to photograph the 'prize' exhibits in the future. But of course other things got in the way, time moved on and impatient farmers and developers decided that their need was greater. Most had no love of history, having seen their vast acreages requisitioned during wartime and their landscape changed for ever with runways, perimeter tracks and huts of every description. Their only bonus was to take over the old wartime hangars and buildings and put them to use for storing grain, combine harvesters and whatever else that is grown and reaped in the Norfolk fields. 'Peri' tracks and runways were largely ripped up to provide more arable land for growing crops with only the bare minimum of concrete left standing to take a tractor or combine harvester.

Some individuals, notably Tom Cushing at Little Snoring, do have a sense of history and having grown up in the area during the war decided to preserve as much of 'their' airfields as possible. Tom later organised a superb museum on his land adjoining the airfield, which commemorated many of the men and women of 23, 169, 515 and 115 Squadrons. I was honoured to acknowledge Tom Cushing's contribution in the book *Confounding the Reich*, which features detailed research and interviews and photos of all the 100 Group stations and locations from November 1943 to May 1945.

Norfolk people probably take the county's rich history and highly arable land with its inland waterways and coastline teeming with bird-life for granted, but its wide open spaces have been fought over for centuries. Now, day-trippers from near and far and holidaymakers from overseas have replaced the warlike hordes of Scandinavia who added Old Norse to the broad Norfolk dialect and introduced many names to the geography of the region. Norwich is at the hub. A magnificent cathedral and proud castle dominate the skyline. During World War Two Norwich sadly did not escape widespread destruction on occasion. Allied personnel stationed in the county came to love the area and some stayed to put down roots. Now the county's rich heritage is under siege from developers and the ravages of the North Sea. At Hunstanton, there is a memorial listing all those killed in the North Sea floods of 31 January 1953. It includes seventeen American airmen from RAF Sculthorpe.

I am enormously grateful to the following people for making it possible to include detailed information in this book. Dr Theo Boiten provided enormous expertise on victories and details of German crews. Bob Collis unstintingly provided his customary expertise and furnished much valuable information on aircraft and crews, often in very detailed and painstaking correspondence. I am no less grateful to the following for their marvellous help and support throughout: Michael Allen DFC **; Jim Avis; Molly Baker; Len Bartram; Derek 'Taffy' Bellis DFC *; Philip J. Birtles; Eileen Boorman; Les Bostock; Bill Bridgeman; Squadron Leader Joe Cooper AFC; Ernie Frohloff; Air Vice Marshal Jack Furner CBE, DFC, AFC; Peter B. Gunn; Terry Groves; Alan Hague, Curator, Norfolk & Suffolk Aviation Museum; Gerhard Heilig; Leslie 'Dutch' Holland; Mervyn Hambling; Sister Laurence May; W.H. Miller DFC; Mosquito Aircrew Association; Simon Parry, Murray Peden DFC QC; Eric Phillips; Don Prutton; Harry Reed DFC; Wing Commander Philip Russell DFC; Jerry Scutts; Group Captain J.A.V. Short MBIM; Group Captain E.M. Smith DFC* DFM; Martin Staunton; Graham 'Chalky' White; Squadron Leader R. G. 'Tim' Woodman DSO DFC; Johnny Wynne DFC; Philip Yaxley.

INTRODUCTION

The Battle of Germany and the Electronic War

In May 1940 when RAF Bomber Command made the decision to begin strategic bombing of the German Reich by night following heavy losses by day, there was little the *Luftwaffe* could do to counter these early attacks. The subject of night-fighting was raised at a conference of German service chiefs just before the war and according to *Kommodore* Josef Kammhuber, who was present at the conference, it was dismissed out of hand with the words 'Night-fighting! It will never come to that!' Hitherto, the night air-defence of the *Reich* was almost entirely entrusted to the *Flak* arm of the *Luftwaffe*. No specialised night-fighting arm existed, though IV./(N)JG2) JG2 equipped with Bf 109Ds was undertaking experimental *Helle Nachtjagd* (illuminated night-fighting) sorties with the aid of searchlights in northern Germany and in the Rhineland. On the night of 25/26 April a Hampden on a minelaying operation near Sylt became the first Bomber Command aircraft to be shot down by a German fighter at night. The *Helle Nachtjagd* technique used in 1940 and early 1941 was entirely dependent on weather conditions and radar-guided searchlights and simply could not penetrate thick layers of cloud or industrial haze over the Ruhr and other German industrial centres. Kammhuber soon concentrated all his energies in developing an efficient radar-controlled air defence system. Meanwhile, RAF bomber crews tried to come to terms with flying and bombing by night. Few people had much experience of flying long distances at night, sometimes in appalling weather conditions, let alone against highly efficient enemy defences. The effort needed to penetrate Germany with outdated aircraft like the Hampden and Whitley in 1940-41 required a deep-seated motivation and a special quality. The Wellington was probably the best of the aircraft available but it was outdated, unable to reach much height over the target, poorly armed and when carrying a full bomb load of 4000lb had a speed of less than half that of a German fighter. To find their way, the RAF crews flew by dead-reckoning navigation and by map reading if they could see the ground. Sophisticated navigational aids would only come much later in the war. Target identification was extremely difficult and it was often only the light flak and searchlights in the target area that led them to their objective. Throughout the summer of 1940 attacks were made on targets in Frankfurt, Wilhelmshaven, Berlin, Kiel, Hamburg, Düsseldorf, Munich and many towns in the Ruhr Valley. The enemy defences, which at the outset had

8

been rather haphazard and not particularly effective, showed a marked improvement and losses mounted.

In June 1940 *Hauptmann* Wolfgang Falck, *Kommandeur* I./ZG1, who had some experience with radar-directed night-fighting sorties in the Messerschmitt Bf 110, was ordered to form the basis of a *Nachtjagd*, or night-fighting arm, by establishing the first night-fighter *Gruppe,* I./NJG1. Falck was appointed *Kommodore* of NJG1 and IV./(N)JG2 was incorporated into the first *Nachtjagd Geschwader* as III./NJG1. From Düsseldorf airfield NJG1's Bf 110s and Do 17Zs undertook experimental night-fighting sorties in defence of the Ruhr with the aid of one flak searchlight regiment. In July Hermann Göring, the *Luftwaffe* chief, ordered Kammhuber to establish a full-scale night-fighting arm. Within three months, Kammhuber's organisation was remodelled into *Fliegerkorps* XII and by the end of 1940 *Nachtjagd* had three searchlight batallions and five night-fighter *Gruppen*. On 9 July *Nachtjagd's* first official victory over the *Reich* occurred off Heligoland when a Whitley was destroyed. By the end of the month I./NJG1 had destroyed five more bombers. At least nineteen Bomber Command aircraft were destroyed from July to December 1940 in the 'Kammhuber Line', as the continuous belt of searchlights and radar positions between Schleswig-Holstein and northern France was known to RAF bomber crews. About thirty bombers were brought down by flak during the same period. During January 1941 eight bombers were destroyed by *Nachtjagd* and in May forty-one bombers were claimed. Bomber losses were running at approximately 5 per cent, so everyone was living on luck after the twentieth trip and they all had to fly thirty operations to complete their tour.

In December 1941 *Nachtjagd* claimed thirteen bombers. Mainly because of a lull in Bomber Command operations, just sixteen bombers were claimed destroyed by *Nachtjagd* in January 1942. Meanwhile, new RAF aircraft such as the twin-engined Avro Manchester and the four-engined Short Stirling began to appear. The arrival of the Avro Lancaster in squadron service with 44 Squadron, which finished converting from the Hampden to the new four-engined heavy early in 1942, ushered in a new era in RAF Bomber Command, which also began the year with a new and dynamic leader. On 22 February 1942, having been recalled from the USA where he was head of the RAF Delegation, Air Marshal Sir Arthur T. Harris arrived at High Wycombe, Buckinghamshire, to take over as commander-in-Chief of RAF Bomber Command from Air Vice Marshal J. E. A. 'Jackie' Baldwin. (Baldwin had, since 8 January, been standing in for

Sir Richard Peirse, who had been posted to India.) Harris was directed by Marshal of the RAF, Sir Charles Portal, Chief of the Air Staff to break the German spirit by the use of night area rather than precision bombing and the targets would be civilian, not just military. The famous 'area bombing' directive, which had gained support from the Air Ministry and Prime Minister Winston Churchill, had been sent to Bomber Command on 14 February, eight days before Harris assumed command. Bombing German cities to destruction was not an entirely new concept. Ever since October 1940 RAF bomber crews had been instructed to drop their bombs on German cities, though only if their primary targets were ruled out because of bad weather. During 1941 more and more bombs began falling on built-up areas, mainly because pinpoint bombing of industrial targets was rendered impractical by the lack of navigational and bombing aids. Harris saw the need to deprive the German factories of its workers and therefore its ability to manufacture weapons for war. From 1942 onward mass raids would be the order of the day, or rather the night, with little attention paid to precision raids on military targets. However, 'Bomber' Harris did not possess the numbers of aircraft necessary for immediate mass raids. Harris selected the Renault factory at Billancourt near Paris as his first target on the night of 3/4 March, when a mixed force of 235 aircraft led by the most experienced crews in Bomber Command, set out to bomb the factory. It was calculated that approximately 121 aircraft an hour had been concentrated over the factory, which was devastated and all except twelve aircraft claimed to have bombed.

During March the first Gee navigational and target identification sets were installed in operational bombers and these greatly assisted crews in finding their targets on the nights of 8/9 March and 9/10 in attacks on Essen. On 28/29 March 234 bombers, mostly carrying incendiaries, went to Lübeck, an historic German town on the Baltic, with thousands of half-timbered houses and an ideal target for a mass raid by RAF bombers carrying incendiary bombs. Eight bombers were lost but 191 aircraft claimed to have hit the target. A photo-reconnaissance operation a few days later revealed that about half the city (200 acres) had been obliterated. The increase in RAF night-bombing raids in the more favourable spring weather met with a rapid rise in *Nachtjagd* victories. In March 1942 forty-one bombers were shot down and in April forty-six bombers were brought down by German night-fighters. For four consecutive nights, beginning on 23/24 April, it was the turn of Rostock, a port on the Baltic coast, to feel the weight of incendiary bombs. By the end only 40 per cent of the city was left standing. The raids on Rostock achieved total disruption. Whole areas of the city had been wiped out and 100,000 people had been forced to evacuate the city. The capacity of its workers to produce war materials had therefore been severely diminished.

Harris had for some time nurtured the desire to send 1000 bombers to a German city and reproduce the same results with incendiaries. Although RAF losses would be on a large scale, Churchill approved the plan. Harris (now Sir Arthur) gave the order Operation *Plan Cologne* to his Group Commanders just after midday on 30 May so that 1000 bombers would be unleashed on the 770,000 inhabitants. Some 599 Wellingtons, including four of Flying Training Command, made up the bulk of the attacking force, which also included 88 Stirlings, 131 Halifaxes and 73 Lancasters. The rest of the force was made up of Whitleys, Hampdens and Manchesters. The majority of the *Luftwaffe* night-fighter effort on 30/31 May was concentrated in the *Himmelbett* boxes on the coast and in the target area. The German defences were swamped by the mass of bombers and *Nachtjagd* crews destroyed relatively few. Of the forty-three RAF losses, it is estimated that thirty were shot down by *Himmelbett* operating night-fighters. Post-bombing reconnaissance revealed that more than 600 acres of Cologne had been razed to the ground. The fires burned for days and almost 60,000 people had been made homeless.

Within forty-eight hours 956 bomber crews prepared for a second 'Thousand Bomber Raid' against Essen on the night of 1/2 June. Again, the numbers had to be made up by using OTU [Operational Training Unit] crews and aircraft. Of the thirty-seven bombers lost, twenty were claimed by night-fighters. On the night of 25/26 June the third and final 'Thousand Bomber Raid' in the series of five major saturation attacks on German cities took place when 1006 aircraft, including 102 Wellingtons of Coastal Command, attacked Bremen. The total of forty-eight aircraft lost was the highest casualty rate (5 per cent) so far but the German High Command was shaken.

A record 147 Bomber Command aircraft were destroyed by *Nachtjagd* in June 1942. From June 1942 until July 1943 German night-fighters inflicted heavy losses on the bomber forces. One of the reasons for the effectiveness of the German night-fighters during this period was *Lichtenstein* B/C AI (Airborne Interception) radar, which had been given industrial priority No. 1 in July 1941. On 9 August 1941 *Leutnant* Ludwig Becker of 4./NJG1 (who claimed *Nachtjagd's* first ground radar-directed kill on 16 October 1940) using one of the still experimental *Lichtenstein* AI radar sets in his Do 217Z night-fighter, scored *Natchjagd's* first AI victory when forty-four Wellingtons of Bomber Command attacked Hamburg. During the first half of 1942 *Nachtjagd* received the first Bf 110s specially built for night-fighting. At the beginning of 1942 German fighter controllers were equipped with early warning radar for individual guidance and the crews trained for the *Himmelbett* method of the *Dunkle* [Dark] *Nachtjagd*. The controller directed the fighter to a position behind and a little below the bomber aircraft with a succession of courses, heights and speeds to fly, until he was able to make him out as a dark shadow against the lighter night sky. Kammhuber's system resembled the British GCI-system [Ground Controlled Interception] and it took full advantage of Bomber Command's tactic of sending bombers singly and on a broad front rather than in concentrated streams. All approaches to Germany and its main industrial centres were divided into *Himmelbett* Räume ('four poster-bed boxes'). The procedure was for one night-fighter to be taken under GCI control in each *Himmelbett* box affected by the raid, while any other night-fighters available orbited the radio beacon at different heights in the waiting area. The first night-fighter was vectored towards the bomber formation until such time as it picked up the enemy in its *Lichtenstein* B/C AI radar, whereupon it was released from control and the remaining aircraft were called up and sent into action one by one. The first four *Lichtenstein* B/C sets were installed in aircraft of NJG1 at Leeuwarden in Holland in February 1942. Such was their effectiveness that by the spring successes obtained through the searchlight and GCI techniques were about equal. British countermeasures had to be found, and found quickly, even if it meant sacrificing a crew to achieve it.

When a British listening station monitoring German R/T (radio telegraphy) traffic picked up the code word *Emil-Emil* and special operators aboard aircraft of 1473 Flight subsequently detected transmissions on the 490 MHz band on *Ferret* flights over occupied Europe, proof was needed that they came from enemy night-fighters. On the night of 2/3 December 1942 a Wellington IC of 1473 Flight was sent with the bomber stream to Frankfurt to pinpoint the source of the transmissions. In effect, the Wellington acted as bait for German night-fighters and the crew were to allow the enemy aircraft to close in to attack and to follow his radar transmissions throughout. A Ju 88 made up to twelve attacks on the Wellington, wounding four of the crew, and the badly damaged Wellington ditched off Walmer Beach near Deal.

As a result of the information obtained, intelligence was pieced together on the new radar and countermeasures were put into effect. A

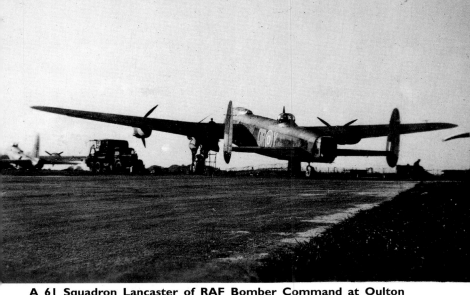

A 61 Squadron Lancaster of RAF Bomber Command at Oulton with a Fortress of 214 Squadron in the background. via CONAM

new, lighter *Window* was produced. Although *Window* was devised in 1942, its use was forbidden until July 1943 for fear that the *Luftwaffe* would use it in a new *Blitz* on Great Britain. These strips of black paper with aluminium foil stuck to one side and cut to a length (30 cm by 1.5 cm) were equivalent to half the wavelength of the *Würzburg* ground and *Lichtenstein* airborne interception, radar. When dropped by aircraft in bundles of a thousand at a time at one-minute intervals, *Window* reflected the radar waves and 'snowed' the tubes. Also, the TRE (Telecommunications Research Establishment) at Malvern, Worcestershire, developed a homer using a receiver known as *Serrate*, which actually homed in on the radar impulses emitted by the *Lichtenstein (Emil-Emil)* interception radar. *Serrate* got its name from the picture on the CRT (cathode-ray tube). When within range of a German night-fighter, the CRT displayed a herringbone pattern either side of the time trace, which had a serrated edge. *Serrate* came to be the code name for the high-level Bomber Support operations.

By early 1943 Kammhuber's *Himmelbett* defences had been completed and the *Lichtenstein* AI-equipped. *Nachtjagd* aircraft were now capable of exacting a toll of up to 6 per cent bomber casualties on any deep penetration raid into the *Reich*. During the 1943 strategic night-bombing offensive, the life expectancy of a bomber crew was

13

Halifax III *A-Angel* of 192 Squadron in flight from Foulsham. via Group Captain Jack Short

between eight and eleven operations. In October 1942 Air Chief Marshal Arthur Harris advocated that Mosquito fighters should be used in the bomber stream for raids on Germany. Air Chief Marshal Sir W. Sholto Douglas, AOC Fighter Command, loathe to lose his fighters, argued that the few available Mosquitoes were needed for home defence should the *Luftwaffe* renew its attacks on Britain. However, on 5/6 March 1943 the Battle of the Ruhr began with an attack by 442 bombers on Essen. The Battle of the Ruhr was fought over ninety-nine nights and fifty-five days, 5/6 March to 23/24 July 1943, and 24,355 heavy bomber sorties were flown. Approximately 57,034 tons of bombs were dropped at a cost of 1038 aircraft (4.3 per cent). Though the flak and searchlight defences around the cities in the Ruhr were by now the most powerful in the Reich, the majority of these aircraft were destroyed by *Himmelbett Nachtjagd*. Between the beginning of March and the end of July, 872 bombers were lost and 2126 were either badly damaged or crash-landed in England. Something dramatic had to be done to curb the *Nachtjagd*.

On 9 May 1943 Ju 88C-6 was flown from Norway to Dyce near Aberdeen after its crew defected during an aborted interception of a Courier Service Mosquito off Denmark. This aircraft was equipped

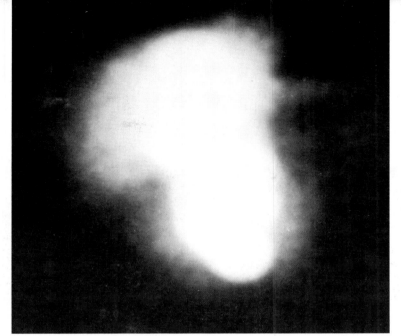

On 1/2 February 1945 Paul Mellows and S. L. Drew DFC of 169 Squadron destroyed this Bf 110 at Stuttgart. Paul Mellows

with the FuG 202 *Lichtenstein* B/C AI. Examination by TRE scientists at Malvern enabled them to confirm that the *Serrate* homing device operated on the correct frequencies to home in on the FuG 202 *Lichtenstein* B/C and FuG 212 *Lichtenstein* radars. *Serrate* could only home in on *Lichtenstein* AI radar and then only if it was turned on. Beaufighters were equipped with Mk IV AI radar, which would be used in the closing stages of a *Serrate* interception because *Serrate* could not positively indicate range. The Mk IV was also needed to obtain contacts on enemy night-fighters that were not using their radar.

The morning after the night before. NF XXX NT252 of 85 Squadron, which was damaged on the night of 1/2 February 1945 when Flight Lieutenant A. P. Mellows DFC and Flight Lieutenant S. L. Drew DFC of 169 Squadron destroyed a Bf 110 at Stuttgart. Paul Mellows

In June 1943, when the German night defences claimed a record 223 victories, the Home Defence Night-fighter Squadrons began high-level, freelance *Intruder* sorties specifically against the German night-fighters. Aircraft fitted with Mk VII or Mk VIII AI radar equipment were not permitted to fly over enemy territory lest their highly secret apparatus should fall into German hands.

At the start of the Battle of the Ruhr, 'Bomber' Harris had been able to call upon almost 600 heavies for Main Force operations and at the pinnacle of the Battle, near the end of May, more than 800 aircraft took part. Innovations such as Path Finders to find and mark targets with their TIs (Target Indicators) and wizardry such as *Oboe,* which enabled crews to find them, were instrumental in the mounting levels of death and destruction. On 24/25 July when Harris launched the first of four raids, code-named *Gomorrah*, on the port of Hamburg, Bomber Command was at last allowed to use *Window* and it was carried in the 791 aircraft. Its effect was devastating. *Window* neutralised the Würzburg GCI and GL [Ground Location] radars and short-range AI and completely destroyed the basis of GCI interception. Controlled anti-aircraft fire was almost completely disrupted at night and fixed box barrages only remained possible. Just twelve aircraft, or 1.5 per cent of the force, were lost. During the Battle of Hamburg, 24/25 July to 3 August 1943, *Window* prevented about 100-130 potential Bomber Command losses. Over four nights 3000 bombers dropped 10,000 tons of HE (High Explosive) and incendiary bombs totally to devastate half of the city and kill an estimated 42,000 of its inhabitants. After the fourth raid on 2/3August, a million inhabitants fled the city. Albert Speer, Minister of War Production, warned Hitler that Germany would have to surrender after another six of these bombing raids. Paralysed by *Window, Nachtjagd* and the *Flakwaffe* were unable to offer any significant resistance. On average, British losses during the Hamburg raids were no more than 2.8 per cent, whereas in the previous twelve months, losses had risen from 3.7 to 4.3 per cent. The new British tactics also combined the use of PFF (Path Finder Force), the massed bomber stream and new target-finding equipment (H_2S). This combination resulted in total chaos to the German night-fighter defence system, which was unable to obtain a true picture of the air situation or control the night-fighters in the air. To try to overcome the crisis caused by *Window*, in early July freelance single-engined night-fighting was hastily introduced into *Nachtjagd* under the command of *Ritterkreuzträger Oberst* Hans-Joachim 'Hajo' Herrmann, equipped with Fw 190s and Bf 109s thrown into the fray in *Wilde Sau* (Wild

Boar) operations, a primitive form of night-fighting in which the pilots tried to intercept and destroy the bombers over the target with the aid of searchlights and in the glare of fires burning below. A record 290 *Nachtjagd* victories were achieved in August 1943.

A deadly new German weapons system was introduced on the night of the Peenemünde raid, 17/18 August 1943. Two crews flying Bf 110s fitted with *Schräge Musik* (Oblique Music) found the bomber stream and destroyed six bombers. This device, invented by an armourer, Paul Mahle of II./NJG5, comprised two 20-mm MG FF cannon mounted behind the rear cockpit bulkhead of the Bf 110 and Ju 88 night-fighters and was arranged to fire forwards and upwards at an angle of between 70° and 80°. *Nachtjagd* also successfully employed *Zahme Sau* (Tame Boar) freelance or Pursuit Night-fighting tactics for the first time since switching its twin-engined night-fighting crews from the fixed *Himmelbett* system. *Zahme Sau* was a method used whereby the (*Himmelbett*) ground network, by giving a running commentary, directed its night-fighters to where the *Window* concentration was at its most dense. The tactics of *Zahme Sau* took full advantage of the new RAF methods. Night-fighters, directed by ground control and the 'Y' navigational control system, were fed into the bomber stream (which was identified by tracking H_2S transmissions) as early as possible,

Fortress BII SR384 BU-A of 214 Squadron at Oulton on 24 May 1944 before Flying Officer Allan J. N. Hockley RAAF and his crew took off on a bomber support sortie to Aachen near Antwerp. They were intercepted by a Ju 88G-1 flown by Oberleutnant Hermann Leube Staffelkapitän 4./NJG3 who attacked the Fortress no less than six times before it finally exploded. Hockley and Sergeant Raymond G. V. Simpson, his mid-upper gunner were KIA. The other seven in the crew survived. Gerhard Heilig via CONAM

preferably on a reciprocal course. The slipstream of the bombers provided a useful indication that they were there. Night-fighters operated for the most part individually, but a few enterprising commanders led their *Gruppen* personally in close formation into the bomber stream with telling effect. Night-fighter crews hunted on their own using SN-2 AI radar (whose longer wavelength, unlike early *Lichtenstein* AI, could not be jammed by *Window*), *Naxos* 7 (FuG 350) (a device that homed onto the H_2S navigation radar) and *Flensburg* (FuG 227/1). This homed onto the *Monica* tail warning device widely used on Bomber Command heavies. SN-2 was a great improvement on *Lichtenstein*, which worked on a wavelength of 53 cm, had a search angle of 24° and a maximum range of 4000 metres. SN-2 worked on a wavelength of 330 cm, had a search angle of 120° and a maximum range of 6500 metres.

Bomber Command continued the offensive against German cities with four raids on Hanover from September to October 1943. Millions of strips of *Window* were dropped, but losses were high. In September, 178 victories were credited to *Nachtjagd*. During October, *Nachtjagd* destroyed 149 RAF bombers and in November claims amounted to 128. Early in November about fifty German night-fighters were equipped with the improved SN-2 radar, which was relatively immune to Window, but only twelve RAF night-fighters and crews were operational, mainly because of the delay in training suitable operators to use the complicated and sensitive radar equipment. RAF bomber losses had now reached a point whereby the formation of a new command was deemed neccesary to alleviate the mounting cost of RAF Bomber Command aircraft and crews over the *Reich*.

CHAPTER ONE

100 (BOMBER SUPPORT) GROUP

On 8 November 1943 100 Group (Special Duties, later Bomber Support) was created under the command of Air Commodore (later Air Vice Marshal) E. B. Addison CB CBE, at Radlett, Hertfordshire. Second in command was Air Commodore Roderick 'Rory' Chisholm, CBE DSO DFC. The task of the new group was to place under a unified command the various airborne and ground-operated radar units, homing and jamming equipment and the special ELINT (Electronic Intelligence) and RCM (Radio Counter Measures) aids that had been fighting a secret war against the German air defence system. In tandem with this electronic wizardry, 100 Group also accepted 'spoofing' as a large part of its offensive armoury and it also controlled squadrons of Mosquitoes engaged purely on *Intruder* missions over Germany to seek and destroy the Ju 88 and Bf 110 night-fighters of the *Nachtjagdgeschwader*. While there were various radar countermeasures that could be activated from the ground, the airborne operations took two distinct forms. One was a force of heavy bomber aircraft flying over Germany and Occupied Europe, carrying a variety of radar and radio 'jamming' equipment, sometimes on spoofing operations; the other was provided from the Home Defence Night-fighter Squadrons. Since June 1943 these had been carrying out high-level, freelance *Intruder* sorties specifically against the German night-fighters. These activities, conducted by specialist bomber and night-fighter crews, and the equipment they used, were cloaked under some strange-sounding code names such as *Serrate*, *Mandrel*,

In November 1943 Air Commodore Addison established 100 Group HQ at Radlett, Hertfordshire and in December moved his HQ to Norfolk, first to RAF West Raynham and in January 1944, to Bylaugh Hall, where the headquarters remained until the end of the war. Previously Addison had commanded 80 Wing RAF, which, as a wing commander, he had established at Garston in June 1940. Addison

Jostle, *Monica* and *Airborne Cigar*. The night-fighter crews who completed a first tour on one of seven fighter squadrons in 100 Group could expect to go for their 'rest' of six months either to BSTU (Bomber Support Training Unit), or BSDU (Bomber Support Development Unit). In the latter, they were still expected to continue flying on operations because the new equipment could only be adequately tested on the job. In those halcyon days that meant 'over the other side'.

The losses among the Lancasters, Halifaxes, Stirlings and Wellingtons were many times greater than those of the *Serrate* Mosquitoes. The task of trying to reduce those losses was a rewarding challenge for all British night-fighter crews. It had to be pursued to the very limit and beyond. Sometimes they saw the bombers being shot down in flames around them. Sometimes they could return to base and tell their welcoming and faithful ground crews that 'they had got one', which meant that one German night-fighter would not be returning to its airfield that night, nor taking off the following night to hit the 'bomber boys'. It was all part of a deadly and sophisticated electronic game in which the RAF, the *Nachtjagd*, aided by the scientists, pitted their wits in an ethereal, nocturnal battleground. One side gained the ascendancy until the inevitable countermeasure was found.

The first unit to move to 100 Group, from 3 Group at Gransden Lodge, was 192 Squadron. Its Blind Approach Training Development Unit had started to fly on the German *Ruffian* and *Knickebein* beams. No. 192 Squadron had been formed at Gransden Lodge on 4 January 1943 from 1474 Flight for the ELINT role with three Mosquito Mk IVs, two Halifax Mk Ifs and eleven Wellington Mk Xs to monitor German radio and radar. The squadron had always been part of the Y-Service and, as such, its primary object had been a complete and detailed analysis from the air of the enemy signal organisation. It arrived at Foulsham in Norfolk on 7 December. Addison's HQ would not move to the county until 3 December, when it was established at RAF West Raynham, eight miles from Fakenham. A permanent HQ, at Bylaugh Hall near Swanton Morley, would not be ready for occupation on 18 January 1944, when 2 Group HQ moved to Mongewell Park near Wallingford in Berkshire, becoming part of 2nd Tactical Air Force. As 2 Group squadrons vacated airfields in north Norfolk, these also came under 100 Group control, as did several newly built airfields in the area. Eventually, the group controlled eight airfields with 260 aircraft, 140 of which were various marks of Mosquito night-fighter intruders and the remainder eighty Halifaxes and Stirlings, twenty Fortresses and twenty Liberators carrying electronic jamming equipment. Late in November 1943 West Raynham became the new home for 141 Squadron, which would become the first operational Mosquito *Serrate* squadron in 100 Group. On 9 December 1943 No. 239 Squadron, which had been training at Ayr and Drem for *Serrate* Bomber Support operations, joined them at West Raynham. No. 239 Squadron had been re-formed at Ayr in September 1943. Its previous function had been Army Co-operation, so that all aircrew for its new role of offensive night-fighting had to be posted in. No. 169 Squadron, the third equipped with *Serrate*, moved from Ayr to Little Snoring on 7 and 8 December. For twelve nights from 4 December, not one heavy bomber had operated because of a full moon and bad weather. When Bomber Command resumed operations on 16/17 December with an attack on Berlin by 483 Lancasters and fifteen Mosquitoes, two Beaufighters and two Mosquitoes of 141 Squadron took off from West Raynham on 100 Group's first offensive night-fighter patrols in support of the heavies. It was hardly an auspicious occasion and became known as 'Black Thursday'. Bomber Command lost twenty-five Lancasters and a further thirty-four were lost on their return to England owing to very bad weather causing collisions, crashes and some bale-outs after aircraft ran out of fuel. All three *Serrate* squadrons operated for the first time on 20/21 January 1944 when 769 aircraft attacked Berlin.

On 5/6 July 1944 Mosquito Mk VIs of No. 23 Squadron flew their first *Intruder* operation from Little Snoring since returning from the Mediterranean, with sorties against enemy airfields. No. 23 Squadron had joined 515 Squadron at the secluded Norfolk base in June after

On 27/28 June 1944 Squadron Leader Graham J. Rice and Flying Officer Jimmie G. Rogerson of 141 Squadron flying Mosquito II HJ911 destroyed a Ju 88 at Cambrai and on 7/8 July 1944 they were flying this Mosquito when they destroyed a Bf 110G-4. via Philip Birtles

When NFIIs began equipping 100 Group in December 1943, the extended operational service with Fighter Command had begun to tell and the Merlin 21s were well used. Finally, in February 1944, all re-conditioned engines were called in and while stocks lasted, only Merlin 22s were installed. via Philip Birtles

flying *Intruder* operations from Sicily and Sardinia. The main role of 515 and 23 Squadrons was flying low-level day and Night *Intruder*s, mostly concentrating on active German night-fighter bases. Although 515 Squadron had been based at the remote Norfolk outpost since 15 December 1943, it had only been introduced to this role early in March 1944. In May 1944 steps could be taken to increase the strength of the ECM (Electronic Counter Measures) and Mosquito Special Duties Squadrons in 100 Group, which now became known as Bomber Support. A lack of enemy air activity in the Western Approaches had permitted the transfer from Fighter Command of Mk X radar-equipped Mosquito NFXIIs and NFXVIIs of 85 and 157 Squadrons to 100 Group. These two squadrons occupied the recently completed airfield at Swannington and officially began operations on D-Day, 5/6 June, when sixteen sorties were flown. Twelve Mosquitoes in 85 Squadron operated over the Normandy beachhead, while four in 157 Squadron and ten of 515 Squadron, patrolled night-fighter airfields at Deelen, Soesterberg, Eindhoven and Gilze Rijen in Holland.

Meanwhile, on 1 February 1944, 1473 Flight, who up to this time had been under the control of OC 80 Wing, Radlett, and whose activities in the main consisted of signals investigation over friendly territory, were merged with 192 Squadron at Foulsham. No. 192 Squadron had transferred to 100 Group from 3 Group on 7 December 1943. The brief was to carry out investigation of German signals from the Bay of Biscay to the Baltic, and along all bomber routes. The amalgamation brought 192 Squadron's strength up to seven Wellington Mk Xs, ten Halifaxes, seven Mosquito Mk IVs and one Anson. On 1 May 1944, 199 Squadron joined 100 Group at North Creake from 3 Group. Some months before, on 22 November 1943, 199 Squadron had taken part in the last Stirling raid on a major German target – Berlin. From this time, an extensive programme of precision sea mining was carried out and attacks were also made on French rail and other military targets. Other useful work was carried out in ASR (Air-Sea Rescue) and, from February to April 1944 199 Squadron's Stirling IIIs delivered vital food and supplies to the occupied territories. In April, 199 Squadron were stood down to await *Mandrel* jamming equipment to be installed in their Stirling IIIs. They would supplement 214 Squadron's Fortresses over the *Reich*. In January 1944 214 Squadron, then at Downham Market and equipped with Stirlings, had transferred from 3 Group to 100 Group at Sculthorpe. *Jostle* and *Window* jamming patrols would form the bulk of 214 Squadron's work and for the ten months preceding the end of the war, over 1000 sorties were completed on 116 nights. On 20/21 April 1944 when the Main Force went to Cologne, five B-17s of 214 Squadron, including one captained by the Commanding Officer, Wing Commander Desmond J. McGlinn DFC, flew their first jamming operation. No. 214 Squadron's role was to jam enemy R/T communication between the *Freya* radar and the German night-fighters. Among other countermeasures, they also jammed the FuG 216 *Neptun* tail warning system. No. 214 Squadron moved to Oulton on 16 May. No. 171 Squadron formed on 7 September 1944 at North Creake, initially with Stirling Mk III and later Halifax aircraft.

July 1944 saw the operational birth of two new and important countermeasures, *Jostle* and the special *Window* Force. The former made its first appearance on 4/5 July and the latter on 14/15 July when all available spare aircraft from 100 Group's heavy squadrons were used. The *Mandrel* screen was used on sixteen nights in August, on several occasions over south-east England, giving coverage to bomber attacks on V-l sites in the Pas de Calais. The greatest success achieved by a *Spoof* Force to date occurred following the Main Force attacks on Kiel and Stettin on 16/17 August. On 17/18 August no major bomber attack took place but a *Window* Force, strengthened in numbers by a Bullseye, and covered by a *Mandrel* screen, headed towards north Germany. The *Window*ers kept on almost to the Schleswig coast, and created in the enemy mind a complete impression that the previous night's attack was to be repeated. No fewer than twelve *Staffeln* were sent up against the bomber stream. An even more important after-effect of this *Spoof* took place on 18/19 August when a Main Force actually did go to Bremen, on a route similar to that of the *Spoof* Force. The German defenders, thoroughly confused, took this attack to be another *Spoof* and left it entirely unopposed by fighters.

On 23 August 1944 No. 223 Squadron arrived at Oulton, formed initially with a handful of B-24H/J Liberator aircraft from the 8th Air Force for operations using *Jostle* jamming equipment. During Christmas 1944 No. 462 RAAF Squadron, the last unit to join 100 Group, and equipped with Halifax BIIIs, transferred to Foulsham airfield, initially as part of the *Window* Force. (On 1/2 January 1945, eight Halifaxes of 462 Squadron flew their first spoofing operation in 100 Group.) October also saw the introduction of *Dina*, the jammer used against FuG 220 *Lichtenstein* SN-2. *Dina* was installed in the *Jostle*-fitted Fortresses of 214 Squadron. This was frequently used in the *Window* Force, as were *Jostle*, H$_2$S and *Carpet*, thereby more effectively giving the simulation of a bombing force. A further realistic effect, also born in October, was created through the co-operation of PFF, which, on several occasions Oboe-marked and bombed the *Spoof* target. (The *Window* Force itself had not yet arrived at the bomb-carrying stage.) The noise of *Oboe*, which had until that time always preceded real attacks only, was thought to give still more confusion to the enemy controller, who, as the 100 Group diarist put it 'was already thinking furiously about many other forms of deceit'. It was also found in October that *Window* Forces could only be increased by deductions from the *Mandrel* screen and jamming forces. It was a point to be considered very seriously, for there was every indication that the enemy was trying to see through the screen, thus making it very likely that more aircraft might shortly be needed to increase the screen effort. So, after the daylight patrols by 223 Squadron came to an end on 25 October, crews began their 'real work', which involved night operations with the rest of Bomber Command. These operations were of two distinct types. In the first, two or three of our aircraft would accompany the main bomber stream and then circle above the target; the special operators used their transmitters, *Jostle* in particular, to jam the German radar defences while the Lancasters and Halifaxes unloaded their bombs. Then everyone headed for home. The second type was the *Window Spoof*, which confused the enemy as to the intended target. There was a radar screen created by other aircraft patrolling in a line roughly north to south over the North Sea and France.

Pilot Officer Kettle RCAF, ball gunner in a 214 Squadron Fortress at Oulton. (Ron James via CONAM)

A group of perhaps eight aircraft would emerge through this screen scattering *Window* to give the impression to the German radar operators that a large bomber force was heading for say, Hamburg. Then, when the Germans were concentrating their night-fighters in that area, the real bomber force would appear through the screen and bomb a totally different target, perhaps Düsseldorf. After several nights, when the Germans had become used to regarding the first group of aircraft as a dummy raid, the drill was reversed. The genuine bombers would appear first and with luck be ignored by the German defences, who would instead concentrate on the second bunch, which was the *Window Spoof*. Sometimes the *Spoof* Force went in first, sometimes last, in an attempt to cause maximum confusion to the enemy, dissipation of his resources and reduction in British bomber losses.

November 1944 produced a new and rather different use of the *Window* Force. With the frequent repetition of heavy attacks on the Ruhr, the enemy adopted a policy of keeping his fighters there, regardless of attempts to draw them away by *Spoofs*. The *Window* Force was therefore

The final 100 Group operation of the war took place on 2/3 May 1945 when a record 106 aircraft took part in napalm attacks on Flensburg and Hohn airfields in Schleswig-Holstein, Westerland and Jagel. Leslie Holland, a pilot in 515 Squadron, who flew this operation, captured the scene in his very impressive painting of the raid. Leslie Holland

used on several occasions to infest the whole Ruhr area with vast quantities of *Window* immediately prior to the arrival of the Main Force from behind the covering influence of the *Mandrel* screen. It was assumed that the enemy fully expected attacks on the Ruhr area and could not be persuaded otherwise. Therefore, the *Window* Force's achievement, which seemed highly successful, was to confuse the enemy so he could not distinguish the bomber track in the maze of *Window* echoes. Still further was he confused when once or twice this tactic was employed and there was no bomber force. Always, however, the *Mandrel* screen was present if the weather allowed, to keep the *Nachtjagdgesehwader* crews in their cockpits, and the controllers at their desks, just in case the bombers were en route.

On 3/4 March 1945 the *Luftwaffe* mounted *Unternehmen* [Operation] *Gisela*, an intruder operation over eastern England suggested by *Major* Heinz-Wolfgang Schnaufer (*Kommodore* of NJG4), the top-scoring night-fighter pilot who finished the war with 121 victories. The operation was to have taken place at the end of February, but details of the plan were obtained and the British made it known by broadcasting the contemporary hit tune 'I Dance With *Gisela* Tonight' on the Allied propaganda station *Soldatensender Calais*. *Gisela* had therefore been postponed until the British relaxed their vigilance, but only 142 Ju 88Gs were committed to the intruder operation, far too small a force to inflict a serious blow. The intruders shot down twenty-four aircraft – thirteen Halifaxes, nine Lancasters, a Mosquito and one B-17. Five of these, including a Halifax III of 192 Squadron, a Halifax III of 171 Squadron, a Mosquito XIX of 169 Squadron and HB815/J, a 214 Squadron Fortress III, which was shot down in the circuit at Oulton, crashed in Norfolk. *Gisela* cost thirty-three Ju 88G aircraft. Five *Luftwaffe* aircraft crashed on British soil and eight other crews were reported missing. Three more crews perished in crashes on German territory, six crews baled out due to lack of fuel and eleven crashed on landing.

When Mosquitoes of 8 Group, Bomber Command, attacked Kiel on 2/3 May 1945 in the very last operation of the war for Bomber Command, a record 106 aircraft of 100 Group took part. Thirty-seven Mosquitoes of 23, 169, 141, 239 and 515 Squadrons made attacks on airfields at Flensburg, Hohn, Westerland/Sylt and Schleswig/Jägel. Hohn and Flensburg airfields were bombed with napalm and incendiaries directed by a Master Bomber. All told, eight Mosquito XXXs of 239 Squadron made high-level and low-level raids on airfields in Denmark and Germany, six Mosquitoes of 141 Squadron made napalm attacks on Flensburg airfield, with fourteen napalm-armed Mosquitoes attacking Hohn airfield. Four Mosquitoes of 23 Squadron dropped incendiaries on Flensburg prior to the arrival by 141 Squadron and seven more from 23 Squadron bombed Hohn with incendiaries

Halifax BIII PN375 FE-X of 199 squadron (note the Mandrel masts below the fusleage) after take off from North Creake for participation in *Post-Mortem*, an exercise which proved the overwhelming success achieved by 100 Group in the final 18 months of the war. via Jerry Scutts

before the arrival of 141 Squadron's Mosquitoes. No. 169 Squadron's Mosquitoes plus four from 515 Squadron raided Jägel. Four other Mosquitoes of 515 Squadron dropped incendiaries on Westerland airfield on Sylt. Support for the night's operations was provided by twenty-one *Mandrel/Window* sorties by 199 Squadron Halifaxes, while eleven Fortresses of 214 Squadron and nine B-17s/B-24s of 223 Squadron flew *Window*/jamming sorties over the Kiel area. Halifaxes of 462 Squadron carried out a *Spoof* operation with *Window* and bombs against Flensburg, while some of the nineteen Halifaxes of 192 Squadron carried out a radio search in the area. Others dropped *Window* and TIs, and some also carried eight 500-lb bombs. Five Mosquitoes of 192 Squadron were also engaged in radio frequency work. At North Creake Air Vice Marshal 'Addy' Addison was present during the take-off of thirty-eight aircraft of the Southern *Window* Force of eighteen Halifaxes from 171 Squadron and ten from 199 Squadron, also heading for Kiel on *Mandrel/Window* operations. Addison expressed his satisfaction at the size of the final effort. One Mosquito was lost and two Halifaxes of 199 Squadron probably collided while on their bomb runs and they crashed just south of Kiel. Only three men from the two crews survived. These were the last Bomber Command aircraft to be lost on operations in World War Two. From 25 June to 7 July 1945 Exercise *Post-Mortem* was carried out to evaluate the effectiveness of RAF jamming and *Spoof* operations on the German early warning radar system. Simulated attacks were made by aircraft from four RAF groups including 100 Group, the early warning radar being manned by American and British personnel on these occasions. *Post-Mortem* proved conclusively that the countermeasures had been a great success.

THE AIRFIELDS AND OTHER LOCATIONS

CHAPTER TWO

BLICKLING HALL

Since 1932 Blickling Hall near Aylsham, Norfolk, had been owned by Philip Henry Kerr, 11th Marquis of Lothian, who was appointed Britain's ambassador to the United States. Lothian liked Americans and his 'democratic' attitude won him admirers throughout the States. He put forward a very good case for Britain's involvement in the war and pointed out her sacrifices and her aims for which they were dying. He also spelled out the dangers a Nazi victory would mean for the USA. The American public, wary of the British (especially those with titles) and many US politicians, were won over by his tolerant, affable approach, which did much to change public attitude towards his country. Lord Lothian worked unceasingly at his task. He made seventeen speeches and a radio broadcast during his all-too-short tenure in the USA. Also, he persuaded British Prime Minister Winston Churchill to write the historic letter to President Franklin D. Roosevelt, which revealed Britain's heavily depleted military strength. Lothian then used a daringly timed press conference in Washington to deliver a similar message to the American public and, in so doing, helped establish the political stage for Roosevelt to enact Lend-Lease and its substantial aid to Britain.

On 6 January 1941, Roosevelt outlined the Lend-Lease programme and enunciated the 'Four Freedoms' principle. The President asked Congress for approval to extend arms credits 'to those nations which are

Blickling Hall viewed from the lakeside. Author

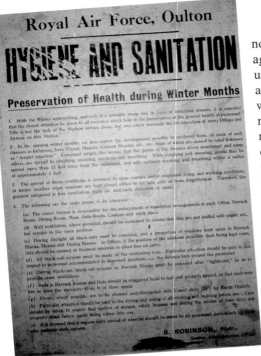

Royal Air Force, Oulton

HYGIENE AND SANITATION

Preservation of Health during Winter Months

1. With the Winter approaching, and with it a possible sharp rise in cases of infection disease, it is essential that the closest attention be given to all measures which help in the preservation of the general health of personnel. This is not the task of the Medical service alone, but one which demands the co-operation of every Officer and Airman on this Station.

2. In the ensuing winter months, we may expect the development, possibly in epidemic form, of cases of such diseases as Influenza, Sore Throat, Measles, German Measles, etc., etc., most of which are caused by what is known as "droplet infection." Expressed simply, this means that the germs of the diseases above mentioned, and many others, are spread by coughing, sneezing, speaking and breathing. With coughing and sneezing, germs may be spread more than 15 feet away from the individual, and with ordinary speaking and breathing within a radius of approximately 3 feet.

3. The spread of these conditions is favoured by close contact, under communal living and working conditions, in winter weather when windows are kept closed either to exclude cold or from forgetfulness. Therefore, the greatest safeguard is free ventilation, fresh air, and early detection of cases.

4. The following are the main points to be observed:—
   (a) The senior Airman is responsible for the enforcement of ventilation arrangements in each Office, Barrack Room, Dining Room, Mess, Ante-Room, Canteen and work place.
   (b) Wall ventilators, where provided, should be examined to ensure that they are not stuffed with paper, etc., but remain in the open position.
   (c) During daylight all black-outs must be removed, and a proportion of windows kept open in Barrack Blocks, Messes and Dining Rooms. In Offices, if the position of the windows prohibits their being kept open, they should be opened at frequent intervals to allow free air entry.
   (d) All black-out screens must be made of the ventilating type. Particular attention should be paid in this respect to personnel accommodated in dispersed positions, e.g. the defence huts around the perimeter.
   (e) During black-out, black-out screens in Barrack Blocks must be removed after "lights-out," so as to provide cross ventilation.
   (f) Beds in Barrack Rooms and Huts should be staggered head to feet and properly spaced, so that each man has at least the statutory 45 sq. ft. of floor space.
   (g) Floors, where possible, are to be cleaned and disinfected with Cresol daily (21°) by Room Orderly.
   (h) Particular attention should be paid to the drying and airing of all clothing and bedding before use. Care should be taken to ensure that clothes of airmen, which become wet during the course of their duty, are properly dried before again being taken into use.
   (i) It is stressed that a regular daily period of exercise should be taken by all personnel, particularly for those who perform work indoors.

B. ROBINSON, Ofldr.,
Station Administration Officer.

Hygene and sanitation notice for RAF personnel at Oulton in one of the former servant's quarters in the upper floor of Blickling Hall. Author

now in actual war with aggressor nations. Our most useful and immediate role is to act as an arsenal for them as well as ourselves. They do not need manpower, but they do need billions of dollars worth of weapons of defence. The time is near when they will not be able to pay for them all in ready cash...'

In a radio broadcast to the US on 9 February, Churchill pleaded for arms support: 'Give us the tools and we will finish the job.' The Lend-Lease Act was passed by Congress on 11 March 1941, when British Commonwealth reserves were almost exhausted. Roosevelt said, 'This decision is the end of any attempt at appeasement in our land; the end of urging us to get along with the dictators; the end of compromise with tyranny and the forces of oppression.'

Lothian had completed his life's most momentous task. He last saw Blickling Hall in October 1940, during a day's break in his busy schedule. That same year, when, after rising costs threatened its future, he bequeathed his beloved Hall to the National Trust. Blickling was the first of almost a hundred great houses to pass to this great institution, whereby, in place of death duties, whole houses and their estates are left to the British nation with their income as an endowment. By then, Blickling had been requisitioned as the Officers' Mess for nearby RAF Oulton and the park ploughed up. Lothian ordered some of the soft furnishings that had been put away for the duration to be brought out to make the officers more comfortable. Lothian returned to Washington in November and died on 12 December 1940 from uraemic poisoning.

When the RAF took over part of Blickling Hall, they occupied the barns to the east of the west wing and used accommodation in the private rooms (now the conference rooms), at the rear of the hall. High in the attics, where seventeenth century maids had slept in small rooms, now slept the 'erks', batmen, and flight sergeants. The Harness Room became a guardroom. Lord Lothian's fearsome secretary, Miss O'Sullivan, nicknamed 'Mrs Dandridge' (after the housekeeper in Rebecca) or, just simply, 'the Dragon' ensured that the RAF remained in their allotted area! It is reputed that the RAF officers were more frightened of her than they were of their CO! Crews of 114 and 18 Squadron were first to use Blickling Hall and then 214 Squadron moved to Oulton on 16 May 1944 and it was the turn of some officers to be accommodated in the mansion. Canadian pilot Flight Lieutenant Murray Peden DFC QC in 214 Squadron recalled what life was like at Oulton and Blickling in his autobiographical classic, *A Thousand Shall Fall.*

We had landed in a veritable Garden of Eden. The officers' living quarters were located in a beautifully wooded area of Blickling Park, a stone's throw from Blickling Hall, a magnificent seventeenth-century Jacobean mansion. This large and beautiful estate belonged to the Marquis of Lothian but a substantial portion of it had been taken over for the duration by the RAF. The grounds were steeped in history. Long before the great Hall had been built the property had belonged to Anne Boleyn's father, and the local legend was that the ill-fated young Queen had spent many happy hours on this spot. It went on to suggest that on particularly dark nights one might anticipate a ghostly encounter with her, walking around the lovely little lake bordering the mansion accompanied by her great mastiff – but walking in the somewhat handicapped manner suggested in the old song, i.e. 'with 'er 'ead hooked oonderneath 'er arm'.

Blickling was our home in effect. Our Officers' Mess was only about 100-150 yards clear of the box hedges of Blickling Hall, and our Nissen hut billets only another 200 yards further on. When we went into Aylsham, or into Norwich, or went away on leave, the place to which we always returned to lay our heads on the pillow was the billets hard by Blickling Hall. When we wanted to have a bath, we walked over to Blickling Hall and up to the top floor of the old mansion where we got a cold (make that, frigid) bath. Oulton, on the other hand, was the place we returned to when we'd been airborne for a while. To go to work every morning, we left our 'homes' at Blickling and rode by bus up to the Flights at Oulton. Sometimes during the morning or afternoon, if things were slack, we'd walk off the station, out past

Details of library opening times during RAF occupation of Blickling Hall which can still be seen today. Author

the guardroom and just across to the opposite side of the road to the Post Office there, where we would buy a cup of tea and a muffin or scone.

Our Officers' Mess was not in Blickling Hall itself, but in a new building which had been constructed on a little knoll 75 yards away. Nevertheless, parts of the elegant old edifice were reserved for our use. We were entitled, I discovered, to take baths in an upper storey bathroom in Blickling. I made haste to take advantage of this luxury, only to find that the water was always stimulatingly unheated, and approximately ten degrees colder than the North Sea. In a beautifully panelled room on the main floor, Jackie Furner, the new Navigation Leader, and the other classical record buffs, soon began conducting sessions of the station record club.

Flight Lieutenant (later Air Vice Marshal CBE DFC AFC) Jack Furner, recalls.

I ran Music Club meetings in one of the ground floor panelled rooms of the Hall. A number of airmen and airwomen attended to hear me talk to a programme of 78s played on a wind-up gramophone with a sharpener at the ready for the fibre needles.

On the very evening of our arrival, some of us drove into Aylsham to survey the local pubs, and after a few beers I wandered across to the blacked-out town hall to look in on a dance being held there. Without hesitation I made a beeline towards a lovely girl dressed in a pink V-neck dress standing across the floor from me. I had known girls at each place before, but there was always the acknowledgement that there would be nothing permanent about a relationship. I somehow knew this might be different. Her name was Patricia; she was 19, just a month away from her 20th birthday. She had a divine figure. She had a pretty face. She was an excellent dancer, easily able to follow my somewhat jerky steps (I whispered two lines in Spanish of *Besame Mucho* as we danced). She loved classical music and played the piano, with a distinguished pass in Grade 8 behind her. She lived in the town square, just a few yards from the town hall. Pat told me some time later that her mother had almost dissuaded her from coming over to the dance that evening (you're out too often my girl). When her father heard us talking below her rooms in Aylsham Square, I understand he said to her mother, 'It's all right, they're talking about Beethoven'. [Jack and Pat married on 7 February 1948].

In the grounds of the Hall, many temporary Nissen huts had been constructed, including one acting as the Officers Mess. One boozy night in that Mess, there was a sudden decision by everybody there to plant somebody's footprints around the semi-circular ceiling of the Nissen hut – merely to convince gullible visitors that somebody had taken a running jump to do it. Well, it was decided that I was Joe, being fairly light in weight. A sort of scaffolding of tables and chairs was constructed, gradually rising in height towards the centre. I took off my shoes and socks. Somebody else blacked the soles with shoe polish and I was carefully lifted up and had my feet planted on the ceiling one at a time. All was going well until we reached the highest point in the centre. The scaffolding began to falter, the structure collapsed. I fell from a great height and my right palm came down, unfortunately, on to a piece of broken glass on the floor. I don't remember much of what followed but the Doc (Vyse) was on hand and took charge. I was losing blood at a fairly fearsome rate to start with apparently until he staunched it. I was carried by ambulance to the Norfolk and Norwich Hospital and was wrapped in a plaster cast for some time. The end result was the cutting of a tendon, a messy right palm and a permanently bent first finger. At home on leave in Southend, I'd be showing my messy right palm to relations and friends and explaining frankly how it had happened. Somebody whispered to my mother that I was almost certainly concealing the real facts and that it was a war wound.

Murray Peden continues:

Oulton had other amenities to offer besides the lovely old

The Buckinghamshire Arms adjacent to Blickling Hall in 1944. Ernie Frohloff

mansion and grounds of Blickling. In a nicely treed fork in the road, a hundred yards beyond the high and stately box hedges that led to the main entrance of Blickling Hall, stood a strategically located public house, the Buckinghamshire Arms. The 'Buck' was to see a lot of our aircrew personnel, both American and RAF, although the day after we arrived I chanced upon another pub in Aylsham, the nearby village, which thereafter became our crew's off-duty headquarters. It was called the Anchor and was run by a pleasant woman named Ena Spink. In a separate little room just at the entrance to the beer cellar she had an old phonograph and, treasure of treasures, a pile of Bing Crosby records. To top it off, as if her friendly presence and the Bing Crosby records weren't enough, Ena usually had a supply of the finest bottled beer it was my good fortune to run across the whole time I was in England: Steward & Patteson's Light Ale, brewed in Norwich by a brewmaster who must have been the unrivalled master of his trade. The first evening Stan and I were able to spend at the Anchor was a memorable nostalgia session. We screwed the tops off a fair number of Steward & Patteson's, and kept Bing performing our favourites all night: *The Pessimistic Character With The Crabapple Face, Pocketful of Dreams, Ciribiribin, Yodelin' Jive, Ave Maria, Adeste Fideles, Where The Blue Of The Night*, etc., etc., etc.

Everywhere we went in England we were well treated by the local inhabitants but for some reason – I suppose because we stayed in that area longer – the people of Oulton and Aylsham made us feel more a part of the community than we had at any of our earlier operational stations. How they suffered us so uncomplainingly is beyond me. God knows they must have wearied of the ubiquitous hordes of uniformed men who established themselves in their favourite spots in the pubs, took over the cinemas, lengthened the queues at the bus stops and in the stores and filled the tea shops and restaurants. In their place I am sure I should have been heartily sick of the invading swarms, many of them radiating the unfamiliar accents of Canadians, Americans, Australians, New Zealanders, Rhodesians and Indians, to name only the exotic dialects that flowed into the area around with the arrival of 214 Squadron. But somehow the great majority of the English carried on as though we were just new families that had lately settled in the district. They went out of their way to strike up conversations with us in the pubs. Within a month we were on a first name basis and playing darts with half a dozen of the regulars in the Anchor, The Dirty Duck (the aircrew name for The Black Swan) the White Hart and the Buck. They invited us into their homes and they came to our mess on the rare occasions when the war permitted us to throw a party.

We discovered the first day we were at Oulton that the aerodrome and the surrounding fields were abundantly stocked with Hungarian partridge and pheasants. A little tactical research in our Vauxhall taught us that as long as one sat in the little van with the motor running, they would not fly. We had been issued with Smith & Wesson .38s some months earlier; so I began to travel about with mine tucked in my flying boot. When I could borrow the Flight Commander's van on some pretext or other, I would prowl the perimeter track for 15 minutes stalking a covey of Hungarians. When we had collected a few, we would take them down to Ena Spink at the Anchor. A day later she would have us down and we would all share a royal feast prepared in her kitchen. All in all, we found the Oulton-Aylsham district a highly congenial one.

We were visited at Blickling by a troop of actors and actresses making the movie *The Wicked Lady*. The film starred Margaret Lockwood and James Mason and focused on the career of a wicked young lady and a dashing highwayman in that era when

Some of the production members and cast of *The Wicked Lady* including Margaret Lockwood and Patricia Roc at Blickling Hall in early 1945. They returned to the Hall in 1946 to film another Gainsborough Pictures' period drama called *Jassy*. via Philip Yaxley

The Wicked Lady, which starred Margaret Lockwood and James Mason and which was filmed at Blickling Hall in early 1945. via Philip Yaxley

carriages and stagecoaches were the principal form of vehicular traffic on English roads.

That stage (a rather ornate old stagecoach) was parked for a few days just outside our Officers' Mess, where it remained until a group of irresponsible Canadians and Americans began making use of it one night – without the benefit of a team of horses. With a little imagination we transported it 5000 miles; with a little more it became the Wells Fargo Express, half an hour behind schedule on the run to Dodge City. Half a dozen well lubricated aircrew got hold of the tongue and the door handles and began propelling the venerable-looking vehicle at a remarkable speed around the little knoll, then down towards the Buck. I was up top riding shotgun with an American navigator and urging the horses on to greater efforts when the producer suddenly burst from the mess and turned pale at the prospect of his rather delicately fashioned replica being battered into kindling. Before we even had a chance to run off our planned encounter with some American aircrew Indians, who were lurking at the Buck and awaiting our arrival at the more realistic pace our horses could muster on the incline, the producer testily commandeered his property and put a stop to the exercise. He had his precious stagecoach (the replacement value of which was probably beyond our wildest estimates) moved to safer storage forthwith.

Undaunted, we turned our ten gallon hats back into wedge caps and returned in high fettle to the mess, where Margaret Lockwood was holding court at the bar, and being stared at by every officer from the Group Captain down. I rise to remark that Margaret Lockwood was worth staring at; yea and verily a real smasher. So captivating was the Wicked Lady that I cannot truthfully say whether James Mason was beside her at the bar or not. I suppose he must have been, but I do not remember seeing him, and I would wager that none of the men present, except possibly the padre, could have testified reliably the next morning on the issue of his presence. Regrettably, Miss Lockwood's visit

During filming of *The Wicked Lady* at Blickling Hall in early 1945, well lubricated RAF aircrew billited there, borrowed the carriage and turned into a stagecoach, riding it around the estate like cowboys heading for Dodge City. via Philip Yaxley

Three Stearman biplanes passing the picturesque Blickling Hall, lake and St Andrew's Church in the foreground. In WW2 the Hall was used by the RAF as aircrew accommodation and the lake was used for dinghy drill. Author

was of short duration. The only people not sorry to see her depart were our WAAF officers, who had fared poorly in the presence of big league competition.

Take-off was late these summer nights. It was just after 11:00 pm when the Aldis lamp's green flash sent F Fox roaring down the flare path. We crossed the coast outbound near Cromer and climbed steadily to 22,000 feet in the clear night air.

I have fond memories of the Castle Hotel in Norwich, although the secluded little green behind the cathedral nearby where Edith Cavell is at rest has also been by far the most indelible impression I have of the general area. I occasionally saw in the darkening sky the spire of the old cathedral looming off in the distance, usually as we swung onto an easterly heading just after take-off and made for the coast and the unfriendly stretches beyond. I never saw it without thinking of that wonderful brave woman sleeping in its shadow. We had read about her as kids when we were at school and I always had the greatest admiration for her courage. I read more about her as I grew up and used to remember, too, that she had spent many summer holidays at the coast at Cromer. And many times Cromer was our point of departure from England on operations.

CHAPTER THREE

BYLAUGH HALL

In December 1943 2 Group relinquished control of Swanton Morley airfield and Bylaugh Hall to 100 Group and moved to Mongewell Park near Wallingford in Berkshire. Bylaugh Hall was finally ready for occupation on 18 January 1944 and Air Vice Marshal Addison and his staff, who since 3 December had had a temporary HQ at RAF West Raynham, were finally able to move in. Squadron Leader Philip Russell, CO 23 Squadron at Little Snoring, used to attend the daily briefings at HQ and he found it fascinating to watch the 'plot being hatched out' and then, on the next day, to be able to see what results had been achieved. Ron Greenslade, who after a short spell attached to the Royal Navy for the invasion was posted from Chicksands to Bylaugh Hall in July 1944, recalls:

At Peterborough I transferred to a local line and the busy little junction of March, and then via my fourth train to a tiny station called Lyng in Norfolk. Here I was later collected with two others and transported by truck to Bylaugh Hall about 2 miles away. Bylaugh Hall, a stately home in its own grounds, had been

Wing Commander Philip Russell, who assumed command of 23 Squadron at Little Snoring on the death in action of 'Sticky' Murphy. Russell attended operations briefings at Bylaugh Hall. Philip Russell via Tom Cushing

Bylaugh Hall near Swanton Morley, Norfolk just after the war. via CONAM

taken over by the RAF as Headquarters for 100 Group. It was not a particularly large camp as there were only seven huts for airmen and eight for the WAAFs. The officers appeared to be in private billets off the camp and the total complement of the station was approximately 150 of which about ninety worked in Signals.

We booked in at the guardroom, which was at the end of a very long drive off the main road, and we were directed through some trees to the airmen's sleeping quarters. There were twelve of us altogether, and we were a very happy crowd apart from a surly Welsh corporal who was supposed to be in charge of the hut. However, as he worked days and the majority of us were on shifts, we didn't see much of him. Amongst the others was Bruce Williams, an Instruments Inspector who, in Civvy Street, had a jeweller's shop in Liverpool with his twin brother.

As most of us were on shift work we were issued with special passes to enable us to obtain meals in the cookhouse more or less how and when we wanted. This could be invaluable at times, especially if we wanted a late supper. At work we were put on a four-watch system and we worked in the Signals Section, which was set in more huts which had been attached to the main Hall. Outside the wireless room was the sergeant in charge of the whole watch. Next door was the teleprinter room (all girls), and beyond that the PBX (telephone exchange). In the Wireless Room were six sets, each with its own call-sign marked above and manned by both airmen and WAAFs with a corporal and assistant behind us for routeing purposes. Our job here was to send and receive Morse-coded messages ground to ground and ground to air but it was not D/F [Direction Fielding] work, which I loved. It was enjoyable work but not particularly satisfying. As it turned out I did not get back to D/F until I reached India where I worked at Allahabad and Palam (Delhi).

There was a corridor from the Signals section to the ground floor of the hall where the Administration Section operated. At break times we used to go there quite regularly to collect a mug of tea and a wad or, frequently, marmite sandwiches. Upstairs was the Operations Room from which the group was organised and where plane routes and positions were plotted on maps but we were not allowed up there. Our Commanding Officer was Group Captain Goodman.

In the evenings, twice a week, we had a film shown in one of the bigger rooms of the Hall and this cost us just 6d. The NAAFI was also a popular place where we would listen for hours to some of the joke specialists. Some of the lads could reel off jokes as good as any stand-up comic. We also had a piano in there and many times we would sing away whilst one of the WAAFs from MT [Motor Transport] played some of the pops for us.

The camp was 6 miles from East Dereham, our nearest town, and I must have walked there numerous times. There was a cinema, which we visited regularly, and a small Salvation Army canteen, which supplied very good meals. Mind you, at certain times you might find yourself joining in with prayers in the evening. Later, a new and bigger canteen opened for both the Americans and us stationed in the area. The counter was always stacked with doughnuts. When we returned to camp it was usually on the liberty bus which left at 10 pm. The liberty bus was a covered truck, which had three wooden forms on the sides and in the back and seated about a dozen people. Any more just piled into the middle or sat on laps. It was always dark by then and as airmen and WAAFs all travelled together it was usually a lively journey. There was another liberty bus, which took us further afield into Norwich now and again. There was much more to do and see there as there were cinemas and a theatre as well as places of historical interest to visit such as the castle and the cathedral.

In the autumn some of us tried to make more money on the land. Some tried haymaking, pea picking, potato collection and currant picking. I had a go at the latter, but it was so tedious that I made very little money and decided one day was enough.

Christmas approached and I went down to the tiny village church of Bylaugh. I thought it would be nice to go to the midnight service on Christmas Eve, as I was not on duty. I got into a discussion with the vicar and with the help of another chap, we arranged to decorate the church with holly and place candles at the end of all the pews. The church looked a picture on the night and the service went very well with a packed congregation.

I was on duty later on Christmas Day when all operations were at a standstill so we had a good time together as we had a smashing bunch of 'oppos' on our watch.

More Americans seemed to be in the area and some of the WAAFs were invited over to their camps for dances, under very strict supervision Iris later told me. We had some real WAAF characters in the WOPs (wireless operators) and later I found out

Derelict Bylaugh Hall in 1994 viewed through the broken windows of a Nissen hut in its grounds. Author

they were billeted in the same hut as Iris. One girl named Beryl would regularly make up her eyelashes with black boot-polish and on night watch after the American dances there were one or two of them quite starry eyed. They told a few stories of their escapades but I was never quite sure how true they were. At the pub the Americans came in and mixed with us and we got on really well together. They were great lads and I saw nights when it was impossible to put another drink on the tables. They had the money and were very generous. The Americans were living for the day, as they were regularly flying over Germany in daytime and they lost many of their pals.

On 3 February 1945 1000 Flying Fortresses attacked Berlin in daylight and most of these flew from Norfolk and Cambridgeshire. Meanwhile, the RAF was doing the night bombing. One night I was put on duty listening out on R/T at a wireless set in an alcove near the Administration Section. It was a very busy night as our fighters had been over the continent strafing. About 3 am they returned only to be followed by enemy fighters. Nobody called me but it was quite a night as I listened in to the comments over the air as the pilots realised they had been followed. There was a real flap on until they were told to scramble, whereupon they landed anywhere they could all over

East Anglia and Lincolnshire. They didn't return to their own bases until the next day.

Back at the camp the girls were all raving over a new weedy-looking singer from America called Frank Sinatra. To me he was never a patch on Bing Crosby. We had one or two concerts organised and one evening Ray Ellington paid us a visit. One of the WAAFs on the camp named Shivadasani was a Jamaican girl. She had a very good singing voice and sang some lovely popular songs including 'It had to be you'. She, too, was a wireless operator, known as Shiwy to us. After the war I read in the papers that she had turned professional and was on a world tour.

About this time a few 'Oak Leaves' arrived at the camp for distribution. These were supposed to be awarded to services personnel for devotion to duty. Many seemed to be retained in the Administration Sections but one was to be handed out in our Wireless Section. After quite a lot of comments and not having a clue as to who had earned it they just wanted to get the job over and gave it to one of the WAAFs. My view of the Oak Leaf award was devalued overnight.

Just after VE Day, Iris and I started to go out together. We were both working the same shifts and as there was now nothing doing in Wireless, I used to stroll down the corridor to the PBX to see her. Shortly after this Iris and I became engaged and, of course, the Signals Section thought we should celebrate, which we did at The Bell in Bawdeswell.

The imposing mansion, which was used as HQ No. 2 Group and from 18 January 1944 onwards as HQ, 100 Group, has now been restored to its former glory. Author

Within a few days I read on DROs (Daily Routine Orders) that I was to be posted overseas. What a time to come, just after getting engaged and the war in Europe being over! I was told to report to the MO (Medical Officer) for inoculations, one of which was to combat cholera, so it looked as though I was going to be travelling a long journey.

It was now the end of July and, after much discussion. Iris and I decided to marry before I went away. I had seven days' embarkation leave so we fixed the wedding day for 8 August 1945 after Iris was able to obtain leave as well. As we had a day's travelling each way for the journey to London, it left us only five days for the preparation and the wedding itself. We left for Iris's home in Mill Hill, London, and soon had invitations out, photography organised and taxis ordered. I decided to marry in my uniform and Iris had a beautiful white wedding dress. We spent hours up the West End of London searching for an engagement ring she liked. We were able to obtain the wedding rings locally quite easily.

News came in of the atom bombs being dropped on Hiroshima and Nagasaki, which was to hasten the end of the war with Japan. There was insufficient time for the banns to be read out in church so we had to go to Westminster Abbey and paid £2 for a special licence. The day after the wedding we had to say our goodbyes and return to Bylaugh Hall.

Next day, VJ Day was announced so I was beginning to wonder if I really would be going overseas after all. I hadn't a lot to celebrate and vaguely remember the day. The following morning I finished my packing and said goodbye to Iris and all my Bylaugh friends. It had been a good camp with many happy memories.

CHAPTER FOUR

FOULSHAM

Construction of Foulsham airfield, 15 miles north-west of Norwich in the parishes of Wood Norton and Foulsham and a half mile north of the village of the same name, began in 1941 and was almost complete by the late summer of 1942. Three concrete runways, the main one of 1900 yards, one of 1400 yards and one of 1350 yards, a perimeter track and thirty-seven pan-type hardstandings, two hangars, a control tower and associated buildings built mainly by Kirk & Kirk Ltd were erected. Domestic sites for 2135 airmen and 355 WAAFs were dispersed in farmland south of the Skitfield road to the east of the airfield and the bomb dump was located off the south-west side. Eventually, seven hangars – six T2s and a B1 – were erected on the main technical area on the east side of the airfield. Another T2 was built on the south-west side near Wades Farm and two more T2s on the south-east corner by Millhill Farm. (Five of the hangars were built during 1943-4 for use by 12 Maintenance Unit for assembling and storing Horsa gliders. In May 1942 the airfield was allocated to 2 Group, Bomber Command. During June to August 1942 Foulsham was temporarily allocated to the US 8th Air Force as Station B.13, but no American units were based here. In October, Foulsham became the operational base of 98 and 180

Aerial view of Foulsham airfield in the 1970s. Author

Aerial view of Foulsham control tower in the 1970s. The tower has since been demolished. Author

Squadrons equipped with the North American Mitchell. For a few days in April 1943 a captured Ju 88A (EE205) and He 111K (AW177) were based here. On all their flights they had an escort of two Spitfires. About forty Horsa raiders were stored at Foulsham in the second half of 1943 under 12 Glider Maintenance Section. No. 2 Group transferred to the 2nd Tactical Air Force on 1 June 1943 and in mid-August 98 and 180 Squadrons moved to Dunsfold in Surrey. Foulsham passed to 3 Group on 1 September 1943 when 514 Squadron arrived with radial-engined Lancaster B.II bombers and two weeks later 1678 Heavy Conversion Unit arrived from Little Snoring to train the crews of 514 Squadron. The first operational raid by 514 Squadron was on the night of 2/3 November when two aircraft were despatched to Düsseldorf and four laid mines near the Friesian Isles. On 23 November both units moved to Waterbeach after only six operations to make way for 100 Group tenure.

The first unit to move to 100 Group, from 3 Group at Gransden Lodge, was 192 Squadron. Its Blind Approach Training Development Unit had started to fly on the German *Ruffian* and *Knickebein* beams. No. 192 Squadron had been formed at Gransden Lodge on 4 January 1943 from 1474 Flight for the ELINT role (Electronic Intelligence) with three Mosquito Mk IVs, two Halifax Mk Ifs and eleven Wellington Mk Xs to monitor German radio and radar. The squadron had always been part of the Y-Service and, as such, its primary object had been a

46

complete and detailed analysis from the air of the enemy signals organisation. It arrived at Foulsham in Norfolk on 25 November 1943 from Feltwell with Halifax, Wellington X and Mosquito IV aircraft, which were used in the ELINT role. On 7 December the station and 192 Squadron came under the control of 100 (Bomber Support) Group. One of the Mosquitoes noted at this time was DZ410, coded DT-K. On 7 December 1473 (SD) Flight arrived from Little Snoring with Mosquitoes and Ansons and became C Flight of 192 Squadron. The aircraft of 192 Squadron were fitted with receiving equipment for intercepting German radar transmissions (including *FuG 200* and *Würzburg*).

192 Squadron crest.
via G/C Jack Short

On 1 February 1944, 1473 Flight, who up to this time had been under the control of OC 80 Wing, Radlett, and whose activities consisted mainly of signals investigation over friendly territory, were merged with 192 Squadron at Foulsham. The brief was to carry out investigation of German signals from the Bay of Biscay to the Baltic and along all

Wellington X of 192 Squadron with an elephant motif. via CONAM

Wellington X *A Virgin's Prayer* **of 192 Squadron. (via CONAM)**

bomber routes. The amalgamation brought 192 Squadron's strength up to seven Wellington Mk Xs, ten Halifaxes, seven Mosquito Mk IVs and one Anson. On 20 February, the Halifax Mk II was changed to Mk III and later Mk Vs were used. The Intelligence Officer at the station, Squadron Leader A. N. Banks, recalls: 'Mosquitoes in 192 Squadron were used to monitor the frequencies being used by ground control of German night-fighters and also to record the verbal instructions used in night-fighter control.'

At 0900 hrs on 9 April 1944 the station narrowly escaped disaster when two USAAF Liberators collided almost directly overhead and some of the blazing wreckage fell perilously close to the bomb dump. In 1944 Foulsham had FIDO fog-dispersal system installed on its main runway, the only airfield in Norfolk to do so. On 27 April at 0325 hours Mosquito IV DZ377 of 192 Squadron touched down in bad visibility. Behind the Mosquito was a 192 Squadron Halifax III, flown by Flight Sergeant H. P. Gibson whose R/T had failed, and on landing he collided with the Mosquito. The RAF Form 1180 (Accident Record Card) recorded that the 'steady green' that was flashed to the Mosquito should not have been given and the pilot should not have been at 500 feet in the funnel or have accepted the steady green as permission to land. The Committee of Investigation concluded that the accident was due to 'juxtaposition of aircraft in the funnel. No navigation lights owing to air raid warning and the Halifax's R/T being u/s. SFCO [Senior Flying Control Officer] posted and reduced – not considered competent.' Banks adds, 'They both came in to land at the same time. They made a good landing and no one was injured. As a matter of fact, the crew of the

Halifax were entirely unaware that their aircraft had landed on top of the Mosquito until they got out of the plane.' A second Mosquito in 192 Squadron, attacked by enemy aircraft over France and badly damaged, managed to crash-land at Friston on returning.

In May the Bomber Support Development Unit, which had been formed at West Raynham on 10 April 1944 under the command of Wing Commander R. F. H. Clerke DFC for trials and development work on radar and various gadgets carried by the bomber support aircraft of 100 Group, moved to Foulsham. Aircraft flown by the unit included a mix of Mosquitoes, Stirlings, Halifaxes, Beaufighters and Liberators.

D-Day saw 192 Squadron in a new operational role. A constant patrol was maintained between Cap Gris Nez and the Cherbourg area to see if the enemy was using the centimetric band for radar, all the known enemy radars being effectively jammed. No positive results were obtained, but centimetric investigations continued right up until the end of the war. At a later date, it was confirmed by the *Y-Service* that the enemy was indeed using centimetric radar and it was believed that it was in fact captured 'friendly' equipment. No. 192 Squadron used sound recorders, both on film and on wire, on investigations into the enemy's radar secrets. It had always played an important part in the interception of enemy VHF R/T and W/T (wireless telegraphy) traffic, both air-to-air, and air-to-ground. Its value was doubly increased from D-Day onwards due to the old question of optical range and such transmissions being outside the normal interception of a *Y-Service* ground listening station.

Crew of Wellington X *B-Bulldog* of 192 Squadron. via CONAM

Halifax III *Sleepy Gal* of 192 Squadron. via Group Captain Jack Short

A sound recorder also played a very important part in establishing the use by the enemy of the *Bernardine Gerdte*, a complicated system, ground-to-air, involving the transmission of *Hellschreiber* traffic, operative only for about ten seconds a minute. Without a sound recorder this particular type of transmission could not have been broken down. Sound recordings were also of considerable assistance in assessing the efficiency of friendly RCM. Sound recordings made of RAF countermeasures, with the actual signal as it was being jammed in the background, meant that the efficiency of the jammers could be assessed. Cameras such as Leica, Contax, Kodak Cine and Bell and Howell were also used. The duration of certain enemy transmissions being so short, it was not always possible for a detailed analysis of a signal to be made by the special operator, but in many instances the duration of the signal did permit a photographic record to be made, enabling further information to be obtained. Cine cameras played a very important part in establishing the polar diagrams of enemy radar transmitters. Some very good results were obtained on the *Jagdschloss* type of transmitter.

On 12 July 1944 Halifax M5638 of 192 Squadron overshot the runway with an engine feathered and wrecked its undercarriage. Between September 1944 and February 1945 two two-seater USAAF P-38J Lightnings were attached to 192 Squadron for ELINT work. The second crewmember operated special equipment in the nose of the aircraft. One of the P-38s is known to have been lost on operations. These aircraft were painted grey overall and carried no unit markings. On 24 December 1944 the BSDU moved to Swanton Morley and was replaced by 462 (RAAF) Squadron flying Halifax B.III bombers. After training, this squadron operated in the RCM role, which included dropping *Window* as well as carrying bombs on some raids.

In the investigation for signals in connection with the V-2, assistance was given by the 8th Air Force, which had already detached a flight of four P-38J Lightnings to Foulsham, arriving on 24 August under the command of Captain Kasch. (In July 1944, an ELINT P-38 of the 7th Photographic Group (Reconnaissance) arrived at Foulsham to operate alongside 192 Squadron.) A total of four P-38s was eventually based at Foulsham for daytime *Ferret* sorties. (One P-38, crewed by Captain Fred B. Brink Jr and 2/Lieutenant Francis Kunze, was lost on 26 October 1944. In March 1945, when the 36th Bomb Squadron assumed all RCM tasks for the 8th Air Force, the three surviving Lightnings were relocated to Alconbury.) Although V-2 jamming proved impossible, during August, 192 Squadron had some success when it found and established the identity of an enemy radar transmission on 36.2 MHz. By means of a *Fuge 16* homing loop, which was fitted to one of the Wellingtons, homing runs were made and its site on the coast of north-west Holland established.

On 5 October 1944, Mosquito Mk IVs of 192 Squadron flew over enemy territory in an attempt to pick up *FuG 200* transmissions and, the following night, checked on the density and characteristics of German AI on 90 MHz, while another Mosquito crew carried out *Jostle* jamming of enemy VHF signals. On 19 October a Mosquito of 192 Squadron flew to Stuttgart to try and discover low frequency Würzburg signals and on 30 October another Mosquito was despatched to Berlin to determine if *FuG 216* or *FuG 217 Neptun* could be intercepted. On 2/3 November five Mosquitoes of 192 Squadron listened in on German radio communications. On 4 December, a Mosquito flew to Karlsrühe to

Mosquito BIV DZ535 of 192 Squadron flown by Flight Lieutenant Roach RAAF DFC and Flying Officer Hank Cooper DSO DFC which crash landed in a field on one engine at Briston, Norfolk and went through a hedge. 'Hank' Cooper Collection

Flight Lieutenant Roach RAAF DFC and Flying Officer Hank Cooper DSO DFC of 192 Squadron in front of a Mosquito B.IV 'M'.

determine whether coastal observation units were being used on inland flak control.

On 21/22 November 1944 a Halifax III of 192 Squadron, flown by Warrant Officer B. H. Harrison, was shot down by fighter attack during an operation to the marshalling yards at Aschaffenburg, Germany. The navigator, Sergeant Stan Wharton and Jack C. Smith RAAF, the wireless operator, were made PoWs. Harrison was killed in the crash. Sergeant R. B. Hales, the flight engineer, and Bloomfield, after first being apprehended by villagers, were handed over to the police. Later, the two fliers were taken under guard by a party of *Volkssturm* (Home Guard) who, en route to Erbach, murdered them in cold blood. Two of the perpetrators died in a car crash three weeks later, one committed suicide and four more were later given sentences of fifteen, twelve, seven and five years.

On the night of 12/13 December 1944, 592 bombers attacked Essen and Osnabrück. (Six aircraft, or 1 per cent of the force, failed to return.) Ninety-one aircraft were despatched from 100 Group. No. 192 Squadron played its first operational role as an airborne jammer when the first Mosquito fitted with two channels of *Piperack* operated. (In time, all the squadron's Mosquitoes would be fitted with *Piperack*. The aircraft played a dual role. Signals investigation continued to and from the target; *Piperack* itself was used over the target.) During Christmas 1944, 462 (RAAF) Squadron, the last unit to join 100 Group, and equipped with Halifax B.IIIs, transferred to Foulsham airfield, initially as part of the *Window* Force. The reaction of crews commanded by Wing Commander David J. Shannon DFC (the award was for his part on the famous Dambusters raid) to being taken off bombing operations in 4 Group in order to drop strips of silver paper in 100 Group is unknown. But bombs were carried until installation of *Airborne Cigar* was completed in March and the Aussies could begin jamming operations over the *Reich*! They certainly brought an infusion of humour to Foulsham as Jack A. V. Short recalls:

Like most Nissen huts, those at RAF Foulsham were equipped with two large black cast-iron coke burning stoves for heating. During winter these were barely adequate to warm this living/sleeping accommodation. To generate maximum heat it was necessary to burn plenty of wood, acquired by whatever means, and to keep the chimney pipe out through the roof clear of soot. Both the former and latter were executed with aplomb by the members of one hut occupied by members of 462 Squadron RAAF. Collecting the timber was a doddle. On the face of it chimney cleaning presented the greater challenge. However, this was accomplished with equal dexterity by lighting a fire, dropping a Very cartridge into the stove, abandoning the hut and waiting for the massive 'whoosh' as the cartridge exploded, driving the soot and contents of the fire out through the top of the chimney pipe! After which the fire roared away without hindrance for a couple of months! A somewhat vicious trick carried out by the Australians returning from an evening drinking session was to select a bed occupied by someone less than generally popular. The perpetrators would then pour Ronsonol lighter fuel across the blanket at the bottom of the bed. This would be ignited at the same time as the sleeping occupant was awakened with the cry, 'Excuse me mate but your bed is on fire!

On 23/24 February a 239 Squadron Mosquito flown by Flight Sergeant Twigg and his navigator, Flight Sergeant Turner, overshot as it was landing on the FIDO strip at Foulsham and hit a parked Halifax. Twigg was killed and Turner was injured. Worse, four Halifaxes of 462 (RAAF) Squadron failed to return to the airfield after a *Window* operation in the Neuss area of the Ruhr by ten Halifaxes of the Squadron, each carrying three 750-lb incendiary clusters and a 500-lb GP (General Purpose) bomb. One of the Halifaxes lost was MZ447 A-Able flown by Flight Lieutenant Allan J. Rate RAAF and his six crew on their twenty-ninth operation. It carried a 'spare bod', Flying Officer D. N. Kehoe RAAF, the new Squadron Bombing Leader. Flight Sergeant

Reg Gould, the air bomber, was the only crewmember to survive. He was soon taken prisoner and placed in a vehicle with three downed aircrew from Flight Lieutenant F. H. Ridgewell's Halifax. Sergeant R. C. Hodgson, the flight engineer, who was about nineteen years old, was injured. Flying Officer J. R. Boyce RAAF, the wireless operator, was badly burned. His parachute had been on fire. It was obvious that he was in very severe pain as the smell of his burnt flesh was terrible. Later Gould learned that the third person was Pilot Officer W. J. Mann, who navigated for Ridgewell's crew. By the war's end, 462 RAAF Squadron had lost twenty-three Australian and twenty RAF aircrew on *spoof* and jamming operations.

On 3/4 March 1945, RAF Bomber Command sent two large forces of bombers to Germany, 234 aircraft to raid the synthetic oil plant at Kamen and a further 222 aircraft to attack an aqueduct on the Dortmund-Ems canal at Ladbergen. Altogether, 100 Group dispatched sixty-one aircraft on RCM sorties this night to jam the German radar and radio networks and thus hamper the enemy flak and night-fighter defences. One of the aircraft was a 192 Squadron Halifax piloted by Wing Commander Donaldson. His tail gunner was Gunnery Leader Jack Short, who had returned to Foulsham in February after a Gunnery Leader's Course at Catfoss:

> We went out in daylight, surrounded by Lancasters of 5 Group – the 'Death or Glory Boys', who were to punch a hole in the canal. Our lone Halifax caused a great deal of interest. They must have wondered if we had the right raid! It was a comfortable feeling though being with all these aircraft in daylight. At the target there was altostratus at 15,000 feet; bloody annoying because the searchlights silhouetted us against the cloud and we were picked up by the ack-ack. I saw three Lancs go down, one fairly close, in flames. [From these two raids, seven Lancasters were lost.] We were keyed up. Donaldson tipped the Halifax on one wing to look underneath for fighters. If suddenly your right wing crumples... but we encountered no opposition, and we headed back to Foulsham at 10,000 feet.

This night the *Luftwaffe* mounted *Unternehmen* [Operation] *Gisela*. The Ju 88s penetrated the airspace over some of the 100 Group stations, Foulsham included. Jack Short continues:

> I will always remember the WAAF girl's voice in the Foulsham tower, 'You're clear to circle and orbit at 6,000 feet,' she said. Donaldson was the last back and we were the top of the stack. There were four to five more Halifaxes underneath at 500-feet intervals. We could see Foulsham airfield illuminated below.

Nose art of Halifax III *B-Babe* of 192 Squadron at Foulsham. via CONAM

Donaldson started a left orbit. I suddenly saw a two-second set of tracer well beneath the aircraft, then more, in one direction. Then a ball of fire. This poor girl on the R/T screamed, 'Bandits! Bandits!' The airfield lights were doused. She yelled out Weston Zoyland, the diversion airfield, in plain language. Then there was total silence.

The aircraft Jack Short had seen was Halifax Mk III LV955 'C' of 192 Squadron, piloted by Flying Officer E. D. 'Robbie' Roberts. Roberts had taken off from RAF Foulsham at 2000 hours for a lone ELINT operation over the North Sea to search for possible navigational aids, which it was thought might be associated with air-launched V-1s and their guidance to targets in the UK. The Halifax carried out its assigned task and returned to Norfolk. At about 0100 hours, the two Main Forces were also over-flying the area. *G-George* arrived back over

Foulsham. Robbie Roberts recalls:

When we arrived, the airfield lighting was on and after calling the tower for permission to land I began to lose height down into the circuit when given the OK to 'pancake'. My navigation lights were on and wheels lowered. The next thing, a cry over the radio from the control tower said, 'Bandits overhead!' and the lighting went out on the ground. I hit the switch to turn off the navigation lights and turned away from the circuit.

Roberts was instructed to turn to starboard. Whilst flying at an altitude of 1200 feet, a Ju 88 night-fighter attacked. The pilot continues:

The attack appeared to come from below us. It looked like that from the tracer. The aircraft was hit and both inner engines were put out of action and the aircraft caught fire. Sergeant Ken Sutcliffe, the mid-upper gunner, reported streams of flame as the petrol leaking from the wing tanks ignited. I thought that there would be a chance for some to escape by parachute and gave the order for an emergency parachute escape, provided I could keep the aircraft under some sort of control. [Only Flying Officer R. C. Todd, the special wireless operator, was able to bale out successfully, injured.] At 1000 feet I ordered all the crew back to the normal crash positions and told them to sit tight as it was too low by then to attempt any further parachute escapes. We suffered a further attack and this resulted in the extremely messy death of the wireless operator, Warrant Officer William Clementson, who was in his crash position in the cockpit, and also the disintegration of the instrument panel. I grappled with the controls and tried to maintain some sort of stability, looking for a field in which I could make a crash-landing. I can remember passing over some trees in the boundary of the field and pulling everything back in my lap in an endeavour to make a belly-landing, which apparently did come off.

G-George crash-landed in flames at Ainlies Farm, Fulmodeston, near the Mosquito fighter base at Little Snoring, setting a haystack and two huts on fire. Warrant Officer William Darlington, navigator, Sergeant John Anderson, flight engineer, and Flight Sergeant Reginald Holmes, air bomber, were found dead in the burnt-out wreckage. Only two men survived, dragged clear by local people; Roberts suffered a crush-fractured spine and burns and did not regain consciousness until two weeks later. After treatment at RAF Hospital Ely and East Grinstead, where he underwent plastic surgery under the famous Sir Archibald McIndoe and thus became a member of the famous Guinea Pig Club, he

In between the hangars at Foulsham are several ex-wartime buildings, either disused or in use by local industry. Above the doorway of one of the buildings are the painted letters, 'Ground Equipment'. Author

Hangar reflected in a hut window at Foulsham. Author

Three hangars remain intact at Foulsham. Author

Crew of Wellington X 'F' *Miss Carriage* of 192 Squadron. via CONAM

was discharged from the RAF in 1947. The mid-upper gunner, Sergeant Ken Sutcliffe, survived with burns to his body and face. The aircraft was almost completely destroyed. The rear gunner, thirty-four year old Sergeant Richard Grapes, was found dead with his parachute unopened, either killed due to lack of altitude, or enemy fire as he jumped. Jack Short accompanied his coffin to Liverpool.

On 25 April special permission was granted for a single Halifax of 192 Squadron, with a full bomb load, to join 359 Lancasters on a raid on the SS barracks and Hitler's bunker at the Eagle's Nest. By early 1945

Halifax BIII LW635 DT-*D* for *Dickie* of 192 Squadron, which crash-landed in a field near Foulsham at 1645 hours on 23 May 1944 with its port inner out. via CONAM

the aircraft of 192 Squadron were being fitted with jamming equipment, which included *Piperack* and *Dinah* and supported the Main Force bombing raids. In April 1945 Mosquito PRXVIs replaced the B.IVs in 192 Squadron. On 2/3 May 1945, the very last operation of the war for Bomber Command was flown against airfields at Flensburg, Hohn, Westerland/Sylt and Schleswig/Jägel. Hohn and Flensburg airfields would be bombed with napalm and incendiaries directed by a Master Bomber. Support for the night's operations included ten Halifaxes of 462 Squadron, which would carry out a *Spoof* operation with *Window* and drop bombs against Flensburg while some of the nineteen Halifaxes of 192 Squadron carried out a radio search in the area. Others dropped *Window* and TIs, and some also carried eight 500-lb bombs. Five Mosquitoes of 192 Squadron were also engaged in radio frequency work.

A total of forty-five Bomber Command aircraft failed to return or were lost in crashes during operations flown from Foulsham (ten Mitchells, two Wellingtons, twenty-six Halifaxes, five Mosquitoes and two Lancasters). By 22 August 1945 when it disbanded, 192 Squadron was flying Mosquito PRVI, Halifax B.III, Anson I and Oxford II aircraft. Most of these remained at Foulsham, where they were prepared for the

Canadian radar personnel at Foulsham leaving the local railway station on the first part of their journey home in 1945. L-R: Lou Orbane, Ray Graham, Sergeant Bearman, Sergeant Hugh Holm, Corporal Griffith; Corporal G. Hull. Sgt Bearman Coll via CONAM

Radio Warfare Establishment at Watton. On 15 September 1945 Foulsham opened its gates to the public for a Battle of Britain Open Day. Among the aircraft in the display were Spitfire 12.XVI TB625, K2-A of 2 Group Communications Flight; Wellington B.X LP152, AY-B of 17 OTU; Warwick ASR.I HG212, RL-G of 279 Squadron; Hellcat NF.II of the FAA; Stirling GR.IV JC364, 7T-J of 196 Squadron with a Horsa glider; Mosquito NFXXX NT478 TW-B of 141 Squadron and Mosquito BXVI NS797, DT-N, ex-192 Squadron. No. 462 Squadron disbanded on 24 September 1945 and by October the station had closed and was retained on a care and maintenance basis. In the mid-1950s a USAF radio unit was based at Foulsham. During 1960-61 the aircraft of the McAully Flying Group were based at Foulsham as their hangar at Little Snoring had been damaged in a gale and another was being built. Noted there in August 1960 were three Tiger Moths (including G-ANCS), three Hawk Trainers, a Messenger and Tipsy I Trainer G-AFWT.

Mr Wallace Cubitt formed Norfolk Aerial Spraying during March 1976. By 1985 the crop sprayers had left and a light aircraft maintenance facility was established here. By 1985 the runways and other concrete areas had been broken up, leaving just a section on the east side for the light aircraft. Currently, the hangars remain on site, but the control tower has been demolished. One of the T2 hangars has been used to hold bulk grain for an agricultural merchant; another is used by the Department of the Environment to store equipment and yet another by a warehousing company. Parts of the taxiway are used by light aircraft.

CHAPTER FIVE

GREAT MASSINGHAM

This airfield, directly adjacent to Great Massingham village, was built in 1940 as a satellite for West Raynham 2 miles away. In September 1940 Blenheims of 18 Squadron were the first to arrive from their parent station, remaining at Great Massingham until mid-April 1941, when they moved to Oulton. In May, 107 Squadron's Blenheims arrived from Scotland, where they had been flying operations in support of Coastal Command. A short while later Fortress Is of 90 Squadron arrived, but their stay was short because of the poor runways and dispersals and the unit soon moved to Polebrook in Northamptonshire. No. 107 Squadron was stationed at Great Massingham until mid-August 1943, having converted to the Douglas Boston III early in 1942. The Squadron's first Boston operation went ahead on 8 March 1942. Losses were high. In operations from Great Massingham, eleven Blenheims and twenty-six Bostons failed to return from one hundred raids. In July 1943, 342 'Lorraine' Squadron arrived with its Bostons from Sculthorpe, but stayed only a few weeks before moving to Hartford Bridge to join 107 Squadron. Four T2 hangars had been erected – two on the east side of the airfield north of the village and two on the north-east side and a single B1 hangar to the south-east. The Unit Construction Company Ltd now arrived to lay three runways and extend the area of the airfield to the west. The main runway was 2000 yards in length and the two cross runways were each 1400 yards long. The runway and perimeter track construction programme left only sixteen pan hardstandings remaining, so twenty loop types were laid to take the number to thirty-six. The accommodation and technical site north-west of the village at Little Massingham eventually consisted of dispersed sites, two communal, two WAAF, and five domestic and sick quarters. In total, accommodation was available for 1778 airmen and 431 WAAFs.

Great Massingham reopened in late April 1944 and on 3 and 4 June 169 Squadron, which was equipped with Mosquito FBVIs, arrived from Little Snoring. No. 1692 Flight, a bomber support training unit with Beaufighters and Mosquitoes, was also based here. No. 169 Squadron, which flew its first operation from Great Massingham on 5 June, operated mainly on *Night Ranger* sorties and later *Serrate* sorties to seek out any night-fighters operating against Bomber Command Main Force

169 Squadron receives its crest (motto 'Hunt and Destroy') in front of a hangar and Mosquito FBVI at Great Massingham. Joe Cooper

operations. In October 1944 the Central Fighter Establishment (CFE) was formed at the airfield, remaining there until August 1945 when it moved to West Raynham. During their stay at Great Massingham, 169 Squadron's Mosquito crews acquitted themselves well. On 8/9 June 1944 Wing Commander Neil Bromley OBE and Flight Lieutenant P. V. Truscott shot down a Dornier 217 in the Paris area. On 13/14 June Warrant Officer Les Turner and Flight Sergeant Frank Francis in a Mosquito VI took off from Great Massingham at 2320 hours and returned having shot down a Ju 88 in the Paris area. On 16/17 June Flying Officer Wilfred Handel Miller and Flying Officer Freddy Bone destroyed a Ju 88 in the Pas de Calais. On 28/29 June Pilot Officer Harry Reed and Flying Officer Stuart Watts got a Bf 110 near Mucke. On 5/6 July Flying Officer P. G. Bailey and Flying Officer J. O. Murphy got a Ju 88 south of Paris. On the night of 14/15 July Turner and Francis destroyed a Bf 109 at Auderbelck after setting off from Great Massingham at 2310 hours. A famous night for 169 Squadron at Great Massingham occurred on 20/21 July with the destruction of '100 Group's 100th Hun' when Reed and Watts got a Ju 88 in the Homburg area. Flight Lieutenant J. S. Fifield and Flying Officer F. Staziker destroyed a Bf 110 at Courtrai and Wing Commander Bromley

and Philip Truscott destroyed a Bf 110G-4, which crashed near Moll in Belgium. The squadron was presented with a coveted silver tankard inscribed, 'To the hungry Hun hunters of 169 Squadron', a reference to the Squadron's motto 'Hunt and Destroy'. (On 6/7 September 1944 Bromley and Truscott were killed by flak near Oldenburg during a night bomber support operation for Mosquitoes bombing Hamburg.) On 23/24 July Flight Lieutenant R. J. Dix and Flying Officer A. J. Salmon got a Bf 110G-4 near Kiel. On 8/9 August Flight Lieutenant R. G. 'Tim' Woodman DFC and Flight Lieutenant Pat Kemmis shot down an Fw 190. On 10/11 August Andy Miller and Freddie Bone scored their tenth victory of the war, a Bf 109 over Dijon. Their eleventh victory the following night was not confirmed until after the war, for they failed to return from a patrol near Heligoland when they were hit by debris while shooting down an He 219. Freddie Bone was captured early the next morning and later sent to *Stalag Luft III*. Andy Miller evaded. For four weeks he was sent along the Dutch Underground. Then the network was betrayed. He was among evaders captured at Antwerp and handed over to the *Gestapo*. At *Dulag Luft* the pilot of the He 219 he had shot down in August confronted him!

On 26/27 August Warrant Officer Les Turner and Flight Sergeant Frank Francis destroyed a Ju 88 near Bremen. On 10/11 November Squadron Leader 'Tim' Woodman DFC and Flying Officer Arthur F. Witt got a Ju 188 in north-east Germany. On 30 November Squadron Leader Howard Kelsey DFC* and Flight Lieutenant Edward M. Smith

DFM destroyed an He 177 on the ground at Liegnitz. On 31 December/1 January 1945 Flight Lieutenant Paul Mellows and Flight Lieutenant S. L. Drew got an He 219 in the Köln area while attached to 85 Squadron. On 2/3 January, Woodman and Flight Lieutenant B. J. P. Simpkins DFC got a Ju 188 near Frankfurt while also attached to 85 Squadron. The last victory flying from Great Massingham was scored on the night of 1/2 February, when Mellows and Drew got a Bf 110 at Stuttgart.

On 12 January 1945, two Mosquito FBVIs of 169 Squadron gave high-level and ASR support for a raid by thirty-two Lancasters and one Mosquito of Nos 9 and 617 Squadrons on U-boat pens and shipping in Bergen harbour, Norway. Two Mosquitoes of 169 Squadron flew long-range escort for an ASR operation. Nearing the target, NS998 encountered five Fw 190s. Undaunted, the pilot attacked two of them and damaged one. In NT176, Squadron Leader John Wright was chased by the Fw 190s. Two days later, the first five Mosquito XIXs arrived at Great Massingham from Swannington and joined A Flight for high-level patrols and intruding. Since November A Flight had been flying *Serrate* patrols, while B Flight, which operated FBVIs, used *Serrate* and *Perfectos*. No. 169 Squadron flew its first Mosquito XIX operation on 21 January.

On the night of 3/4 March 1945 Mosquito XIX MM610/H of 169 Squadron flown by Squadron Leader V. J. Fenwick and Flying Officer J. W. Pierce, who were returning from a bomber support sortie to

On 10/11 November 1944 Squadron Leader R. G. 'Tim' Woodman DFC (pictured) an Flying Officer Arthur F. Witt (KIA with Flight Lieutenant T. Redfern on 26/27 January 194. when their Mosquito NFXXX crashed and exploded near Oulton) got a Ju 188 in northe Germany. On 2/3 January Woodman and Flight Lieutena B. J. P. Simpkins DFC got a Ju near Frankfurt while attached 85 Squadron. Earlier in his career, at Little Snoring, Woodman had destroyed thre Bf 110s in February and May 1944 with Flying Officer Pat Kemmis as his navigator/radar operator. Tim Woodman

Kamen, was shot down by a German intruder aircraft during Operation *Gisela*. The Mosquito crashed at The Avenue, Buxton, Norfolk. Both crew were killed. During April 1945, 169 Squadron's Mosquitoes participated in *Firebash* attacks, dropping 100-gallon drop tanks filled with napalm on enemy airfields on the continent. On 18/19 April 1945 eight Mosquitoes of 169 Squadron were among those that flew to the forward base at Juvincourt in France for a *Firebash* raid on München/Neubiberg airfield. On 19/20 April, when three squadrons of Mosquitoes flew a napalm raid against Flensburg airfield on the Danish border, three Mosquitoes of 169 Squadron took off from Great Massingham and flew to West Raynham to load up with napalm tanks for another napalm attack, on Flensburg airfield. No. 169 Squadron was unable to carry bombs on its NFXIX Mosquitoes as well as napalm tanks because they did not have bomb racks or the release mechanisms fitted in the bomb bay behind the cannons. The attack was very successful with good work by the Master Bomber. Flensburg was plastered and strafed from end to end, and smoke and flames made observation of the final result difficult. Further napalm gel attacks were carried out on 22/23 April. Jägel was attacked by Mosquito XXXs of 141 Squadron, three Mosquitoes of 169 Squadron and four Mosquitoes of 515 Squadron. On 25/26 April Mosquitoes of 169 Squadron took part in a napalm raid on Landsberg.

On the last bombing raid of the war, on 2/3 May, to airfields on the Baltic coast, 169 Squadron's Mosquitoes, plus four from 515 Squadron,

St Mary's church at Little Massingham where the Old Rectory nearby was used as a Sergeants' Mess while sites behind and on the right hand side of the road to the Manor housed WAAF camps. The churchyard has a number of RAF graves. Author

raided Jägel. One of Flying Officer Keith Miller's (later to become famous as an Australian Test cricketer) drop-tanks hung up and slewed him to starboard. But for this he might have got caught in the flak. Miller and Squadron Leader Wright both returned to Great Massingham with a tank hung up but landed safely. On the afternoon of 6 May, Flight Sergeants Williams and Rhoden crashed on a cross-country training flight at Devil's Dyke (Spitalgate) near Brighton. Both men were killed. On 28 June Miller lost an engine near Bircham Newton. He extinguished the fire and put down at Great Massingham, where he overshot and crashed. He and his navigator were unhurt. Immediately afterwards, Miller jumped into his car, and headed for London where he proceeded to score fifty-six not out at Lords! During the napalm gel attack on Jägel, Flying Officer Robert Catterall DFC and Flight Sergeant Donald Joshua Beadle of 169 Squadron were killed when their Mosquito was shot down by flak. It brought the number of aircraft lost from Great Massingham during hostilities to fifty-two aircraft (eleven Blenheims, twenty-eight Bostons and thirteen Mosquitoes). No. 1692 Flight was disbanded in June 1945 and 169 Squadron on 10 August 1945. Great Massingham passed to Fighter Command control, which retained the station as a satellite airfield until 1946 when the station closed. In February 1958 the station was sold.

CHAPTER SIX

LITTLE SNORING

This airfield, north of the A148 and east of the Little to Great Snoring road, was built within eleven months by Taylor Woodrow from September 1942 to July 1943 as a satellite to Foulsham airfield. Three runways, the main one 2000 yards and two cross runways, both 1400 yards in length, and thirty-six hardstandings of the loop-type were built. Owing to the gradients of adjacent land, several of these were on a loop taxiway off the north side of the perimeter track. It was necessary to close a road from Thursford to Little Snoring when construction began, as it crossed the site. Two T2 hangars were placed adjacent to the main technical site in the south and another two T2 hangars were erected on the north side. A single B1 hangar was situated off the south-east perimeter. Two of the T2s were for Horsa glider storage. The bomb dump was to the north of the airfield. The camp, dispersed around Little Snoring village towards the A148 road, consisted of eight domestic, two mess and one communal site for 1807 airmen and 361 WAAFs. Though built originally for 2 Group, Little Snoring became operational in August 1943 in 3 Group with the arrival of 1678 Heavy Conversion

Little Snoring marker stone in the village.
Author

Flight and a few Lancaster B.IIs and 115 Squadron from East Wretham (which was to become an American fighter base) with twenty-one Lancaster B.II bombers. The Lancaster B.II was powered by four Bristol Hercules engines in place of the more usual Merlins. No. 1628 Heavy Conversion Flight moved on to Foulsham in September with 115 Squadron remaining until November, during which time its targets included Peenemünde and Nuremberg. In November 1943 115 Squadron moved to Witchford in Cambridgeshire, having lost three Lancasters in operations from Little Snoring. On 8 December 1943 the station was taken over by 100 Group and 169 Squadron. No. 169 Squadron, a recently re-formed unit training on Mosquito intruder/night-fighters for the *Serrate* role, arrived from Ayr and 1692 Bomber Support Training Flight from Drem with Defiants and

23 Squadron aircrew at Little Snoring on 26 November 1944 in front of a Mosquito with the tower, which still stands, behind. via Tom Cushing

Beaufighters. The same month 515 Squadron arrived from Hunsdon with Beaufighter IIs that had been used in the countermeasures role. For over a month these three units trained in the bomber support role.

No. 169 Squadron became operational on 20 January 1944 with Mosquito IIs equipped with *Serrate* and AI MR IV radar and which were re-engined with Merlin 22s during February to March. No. 515 Squadron became operational with Mosquito II and VI night-fighters, using them in the intruder role against targets that included *Luftwaffe* night-fighter bases. On 30/31 January 1944 when Berlin was attacked again, this time by a force of 534 aircraft, 169 Squadron put up two Mosquitoes, including VI-P *P-Pluto*, flown by Squadron Leader Joe Cooper and Flight Lieutenant Ralph Connolly. They returned to Little Snoring having scored the squadron's first Mosquito victory, a Bf 110 in the Brandenburg area. When they landed there were 300 airmen and WAAFs around *P-Pluto*! The full list of air-to-air victories by 169 Squadron while at Little Snoring is:

Date	Aircraft	Details	Crew
30/31.1.44	HJ711/P	Bf 110 Brandenburg area	S/L J.A.H. Cooper-F/L R.D. Connolly
5/6.2.44	HJ707/B	Bf 110 North Sea off England	P/O W. H. Miller-P/O F.C. Bone
25/26.2.44	DZ254/P	Bf 110 South West Mannheim	F/L R. G. Woodman-F/O P. Kemmis
18/19.4.44	DD799	Bf 110 Compiègne	F/O R. G. Woodman-F/O P. Kemmis
20/21.4.44		Bf 110 Ruhr	F/L G. D. Cremer-F/O B. C. Farrell
22/23.4.44	W4085	Bf 110 Bonn area	F/L R. G. Woodman-F/O P. Kemmis
22/23.4.44	W4076	Bf 110 Köln	P/O W. H. Miller-P/O F.C. Bone
27/28.4.44	W4076	Bf 110 South East of Strasbourg	P/O P. L. Johnson-P/O M. Hopkins
8/9.5.44	DD709	Bf 110 Braine-le-Comte	S/L R. G. Woodman DFC-F/O P. Kemmis
15/16.5.44	DZ748	Bf 110/2 x Ju 88 Cuxhaven area	P/O W. H. Miller-P/O F.C. Bone
22/23.5.44		Bf 110 Groningen area	W/C N. B. R. Bromley OBE- F/L P. V. Truscott

On 11 April 1944 Mosquito NFII DD783 of 169 Squadron crashed 1 mile east of the airfield, when it stalled and spun in after a steep turn.

Mosquito FBVI PZ315 of 23 Squadron at Little Snoring in 1944. via Tom Cushing

The crew were killed. In June 1944 169 Squadron and 1692 BSTU (Bomber Support Training Unit) moved to Great Massingham and their place at Little Snoring was taken by 23 Squadron with their Mosquito FBVIs, which had recently been carrying out strafing of enemy airfields and railways in the Mediterranean from Malta, Sicily and Sardinia. On 5/6 July 23 Squadron flew their first *Intruder* operation from Little Snoring with sorties against enemy airfields. The main role of 515 and 23 Squadrons was flying low-level day and night *Intruders*, mostly concentrating on active German night-fighter bases. From September to December 1944 a number of 23 and 515 Squadrons' Mosquitoes were modified to carry ASH, the American-built AI MR XV radar. The aircraft had their machine-guns removed and a small thimble radome fitted on the nose to house the scanner. Both squadrons undertook *Ranger* sorties over Europe until the end of the war, attacking air and ground targets in daylight.

On 2 December 1944 Wing Commander Alan Michael 'Sticky' Murphy DSO*, DFC, Croix de Guerre with Palm, 23 Squadron's audacious and admired commander, and Flight Sergeant Douglas Darbon were shot down and killed over Holland. Another famous pilot at Little Snoring was Squadron Leader Harold B. M. 'Mick' Martin

DSO DFC, who had joined 515 Squadron in April 1944 and was supposed to be 'resting' after flying Hampdens and Lancasters (including *P-Popsie* on the famous 617 Squadron Dambusters' raid of 18 May 1943). He flew many Mosquito *Intruders* and destroyed an unidentified enemy aircraft on 26 April 1944. On 25/26 July, Mick Martin and Flying Officer J. W. Smith flew a *Night Ranger* to Stuttgart and Boblingen and over Knocke in Belgium shot an Me 410 *Hornisse* down into the sea with a burst of cannon fire. On 9/10 September Martin made two strafing runs against aircraft on the ground at Tulin airfield, leaving two aircraft burning. In the Salzburg area on the way home Martin attacked and destroyed a train, which 'blew up in a terrific explosion followed by vivid blue sparks'. Martin flew on, pausing to rake installations at Cheim airfield with cannon fire before moving on to the south-cast end of Lake Constance where a seaplane base was also strafed. At Mulhouse, Mick Martin strafed the marshalling yards and had a pop at railway stations, buildings and lights. The former Dambuster reported that strikes were recorded in most cases.

23 Squadron Air-to-Air Victories at Little Snoring
July 1944 to April 1945

Date	Aircraft	Details	Crew
25/26.7.44	VI PZ178	UEA Laon Pouvron	F/L D. J. Griffiths-F/Sgt S. F. Smith
7/8.3.45	VI 'S'	Fw 190 Stendahl	F/O E. L. Heath-F/Sgt J. Thompson
21.4.45	VI	Ju 188	W/O East-F/Sgt Eames

Mosquito FBVI RS566 of 515 Squadron at dispersal at Little Snoring in late 1944. Tom Cushing Collection

515 Squadron Air-to-Air Victories at Little Snoring
March 1944 to April 1945

Date	Aircraft	Details	Crew
5.3.44	VI	He 177 Bretigny Melun	W/C E. F. F. Lambert DFC
			F/L E. W. M. Morgan DFM
26.4.44	VI	UEA Gilze a/f	S/L H. B. Martin DSO DFC
			F/O J. W. Smith
26.4.44	VI	UEA Le Culot a/f	W/O T. S. Ecclestone
		UEA Brussels Evere	F/Sgt J. H. Shimmon
21.6.44	VI PZ203/X	Bf 110F	S/L P. W. Rabone DFC
			F/O F. C. H. Johns
27/28.6.44	VI PZ188/J	Ju 88 Eindhoven	P/O C. W. Chown RCAF
			F/Sgt D. G. N. Veitch
30.6.44	VI PZ203/X	He 111 Jagel/Schleswig	S/L P. W. Rabone DFC
			F/O F. C. H. Johns
30.6.44	VI PZ188/J	Ju 34	P/O C. W. Chown RCAF
			F/Sgt D. G. N. Veitch
4/5.7.44	VI PZ163/C	Ju 88 Near Coulommiers	W/O R. E. Preston
			F/Sgt F. Verity
10.7.44	VI PZ188/J	Ju 88 Zwishilnahner a/f	F/O R. A. Adams
			P/O F. H. Ruffle shared
10.7.44	VI PZ420/O	UEA	F/O D. W. O. Wood
			F/O K. Bruton shared
14.7.44	VI RS993/T	Ju 34 Stralsund, NE Ger	F/L A. E. Callard
			F/Sgt E. D. Townsley
25/26.7.44	VI RS961/H	Me 410 Knocke, Belgium	S/L H. B. Martin DSO DFC
			F/O J. W. Smith
6/7.9.44	VI PZ338/A	Bf 109 Odder, Denmark	W/C F. F. Lambert DFC
			F/O R. J. Lake AFC
26/27.9.44	VI PZ301/N	He 111 Zellhausen a/f	S/L H. F. Morley
			F/Sgt R. A. Fidler
8.10.44	VI PZ181/E	Bf 109 Eggebek, Denmark	F/L F. T. L'Amie
			F/O J. W. Smith
29.10.44	VI PZ344/E	Fw 190+Ju W34	F/L P. T. L'Amie
			F/O J. W. Smith
29 10.44	VI PZ217/K	Bf 110	P/O T. A. Groves
			F/Sgt R. B. Dockeray
31.12.44	VI RS518/L	Ju 88 Lovns Bredning	S/L C. V. Bennett DFC
1.1.45			F/L R. A. Smith
5/6.1.45	VI RS881/C	Ju 88 Jagel a/f	F/L A. S. Briggs-F/O Rodwell
2/3.2.45	VI RS575/V	Ju 88 Vechta	W/C H. C. Kelsey DFC*
			F/L E. M. Smith DFC DFM
9/10.4.45	VI RS575/V	Ju 188 SE Hamburg	W/C H. C. Kelsey DFC*
			F/L E. M. Smith DFC DFM
15/16.4.45	VI PZ398/C	Ju 52/3M Nr Schleissheim	P/O L. G. Holland
			F/Sgt R. Young
24/25.45	VI RS575/V	Do 217 6m N Libeznice	W/C H. C. Kelsey DFC*
			F/L E. M. Smith DFC DFM

Nos 23 and 515 Squadrons remained at Little Snoring until the end of hostilities. The last operation for aircraft at Little Snoring was on 2/3 May 1945 with attacks on airfields in the Baltic. During a run on Westerland, a Mosquito in 515 Squadron flown by Flight Lieutenant Johnson and Flying Officer Thomason was hit but the pilot landed safely at Woodbridge on one engine. On 3 June 1945 141 Squadron moved to Little Snoring from West Raynham with Mosquito NF30 and FBVI aircraft and was disbanded two months later. No. 515 Squadron was also disbanded at Little Snoring. During August 1945 Mosquito NFXXXs started to replace the FBVIs of 23 Squadron. The NF30 was equipped with AI Mk X radar and its scanner was contained in a large plastic radome on the nose. Both these squadrons also disbanded in September 1945. A total of fifty-five Bomber Command aircraft were lost in operations flown from Little Snoring: twelve Lancasters and forty-three Mosquitoes. Little Snoring then closed as an operational station until December 1945, when it became 112 Sub-Storage Site (SSS) of 274 Maintenance Unit with its HQ at Swannington. The task of 274 MU was the long-term storage of the large number of Mosquito aircraft that had become surplus. In 1947/48 test pilots were flown in from Waterbeach by Anson and Oxford transports. The Mosquitoes were taken out of storage and

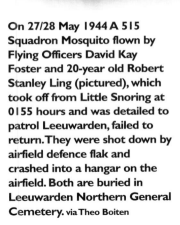

On 27/28 May 1944 A 515 Squadron Mosquito flown by Flying Officers David Kay Foster and 20-year old Robert Stanley Ling (pictured), which took off from Little Snoring at 0155 hours and was detailed to patrol Leeuwarden, failed to return. They were shot down by airfield defence flak and crashed into a hangar on the airfield. Both are buried in Leeuwarden Northern General Cemetery. via Theo Boiten

test flown before they were delivered to the Fleet Air Arm, or other air forces. A few were used as instructional airframes, while others were scrapped on site. Motor transport at Little Snoring included a crash tender and Jeep; the former was on standby while the aircraft were flying, while the Jeep was sometimes used for bird-scaring patrols.

By 1949 about 400 people lived in Nissen huts at Little Snoring airfield. Due to the unsuitability of these huts and a huge demand for housing, the local council built houses on the Holt Road, giving priority to those living in the huts. No. 2 Civilian Anti-Aircraft Cooperation Unit (CAACU) was formed at Little Snoring in May 1951 as a Target Facilities Unit flying Beaufighter TT-10 target tugs, Spitfire LF.16e

P/O Leslie George 'Dutch' Holland of 515 Squadron at Little Snoring, 1944 in front of his FBVI, *D-Dog,* **which is equipped with AI.Mk.XV ASH (Air-Surface-H) radar. FBVI PZ459 assigned to 'A' Flight, where it was coded 3P-D** *'D-Dog'* **and flown almost exclusively by Holland and Flight Sergeant Robert 'Bob' Young.** Leslie Holland

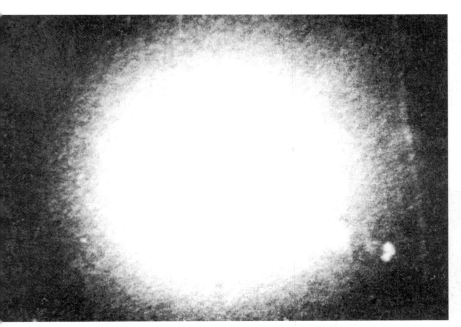

Camera gun still showing the final moments of a Dornier Do 217 which was shot down by W/C H. C. Kelsey DFC* and F/L E. M. Smith DFC DFM at Libeznice 6 miles north of Prague on 24/25 April 1945.
via Tom Cushing

aircraft and finally Vampires, over the Wash ranges. In late August 1951 some ex-34 Squadron Spitfires were delivered to 2 CAACU. The Spitfires continued to fly from Little Snoring, but due to the poor state of the runways the Beaufighters operated from Cambridge airport. The unit moved to Langham in May/June 1952. On 19 March 1953 Little Snoring became a USAF base, being used only for storage and not operationally, closing as such on 18 June 1963. No. 2 CAACU was disbanded in 1958 and thereafter the airfield became redundant. The road to Thursford was reopened in the 1960s using part of the eastern perimeter track as the new route. Local flying interest, sustained by the Cushing family who owned much of the land taken for the airfield, ensured that Little Snoring was maintained for club and private flying over the next three decades. In late 1957 the Fakenham Flying Group arrived from Docking with Tiger Moth G-ANCS, using a hangar and clubhouse on the eastern side of the 'drome. A gale badly damaged their hangar and the Group left for Foulsham while a new hangar and clubhouse were built on the northern side of the airfield. About 1960 the Group was renamed The McAully Flying Group, in memory of founder

Little Snoring airfield in September 1994. Author

member Mr McAully, who was killed in a flying accident. In 1978 the Group had about fifty members and nine aircraft. An aerobatic competition is now held at Little Snoring for the McAully Trophy each year. By late 1983 the Flying Group's hangar and clubhouse had been moved to the south side of the airfield. The runways were broken up, leaving only a strip 500 yards long on the south-west end of the main runway, with a section of pen-track leading to the hangar. The old static water tank is now a private swimming pool. Tom Cushing established a small private museum connected with wartime Little Snoring on land bordering the airfield, but this closed in the late 1990s with the fall off in squadron members. Inside St Andrews church, Little Snoring, are wooden memorial boards listing the sixty-six enemy aircraft destroyed, the seventy-five damaged enemy aircraft and awards and decorations received by the airmen. The eastern and southern parts of all three runways have been removed, but the remainder is retained for flying.

CHAPTER SEVEN

NORTH CREAKE

Sometimes known as Egmere, this airfield, five miles north-west of Fakenham and two miles east of North Creake village, was on an area of farmland known as Bunker's Hill with the camp on the east side. The road from Burnham Thorpe to Little Walsingham running across the airfield site was closed. It was first used during 1941 as a decoy for Docking airfield, which was about 7 miles to the west. In October 1942 Taylor Woodrow began construction of the airfield to Class A standard at a cost of £331,000 and W. Lawrence & Son Ltd erected the buildings at a cost of £336,000 as a satellite station for Foulsham. The technical and administrative sites bordered the unclassified country roads that ran from Wells to Fakenham and domestic sites for 2951 airmen and 411 WAAFs were dispersed in farmland to the east. The three intersecting runways consisted of the main one at 2000 yards long, and two cross runways, both at 1400 yards. All thirty-six hardstandings were the loop type, six on the east side of the Egmere Wells to Crabbe's Castle road, which was closed to civilian traffic. Hangarage comprised two T2

Aerial view of North Creake airfield with the Dalgety site in the foreground and one of the T2 hangars far right in in June 1997. Author

The North Creake operations board which is on permament display at the Norfolk and Suffolk Aviation Museum at Flixton, near Bungay, Suffolk. Author

hangars and a single B1 hangar. By December 1943 the airfield was complete and though originally intended for 2 Group, it passed to 3 Group and finally, in December 1943, to 100 Group, but before heavy bombers could operate additional work had to be made to the runways and perimeter track. Sculthorpe meanwhile took its place in 100 Group's requirements and in early January 1944 North Creake was put under care and maintenance status. From then until April it was used for training by a Mobile Signals Unit and by mid-April a Station Flight was formed using a Tiger Moth (replaced by an Oxford in June 1944).

On 1 May 1944, 199 Squadron (motto 'Let Tyrants Tremble') with EX-coded Stirling IIIs (examples included LJ525 EX-R *Jolly Roger* and 13542 EX-G) joined 100 Group at North Creake from 3 Group at Lakenheath. Some months before, on 22 November 1943, 199 Squadron had taken part in the last Stirling raid on a major German target – Berlin. From this time an extensive programme of precision sea mining was carried out and attacks were also made on French rail and other military targets. Other useful work was carried out in ASR and, from February to April 1944 199 Squadron's Stirling IIIs delivered vital food and supplies to the occupied territories. In April 1944, 199 Squadron were stood down to await *Mandrel* jamming equipment to be installed in their Stirling IIIs. They would supplement 214 Squadron's Fortresses over the

Reich. On D-Day Stirlings of 199 Squadron assisted the landings by simulating a large force of aircraft and surface vessels heading for Calais. On 16/17 June 1944 Bomber Command lost thirty-one bombers from 321 dispatched to the synthetic oil plant at Sterkrade Holten in Germany. Six B-17s of the 36th Bomb Squadron joined sixteen Stirling IIIs of 199 Squadron in routine *Mandrel* sorties to cover the attack. Stirling LJ531 EX-N of 199 Squadron failed to return to North Creake. Pilot Officer T. W. Dale RNZAF, his six crew and Flight Sergeant F. Lofthouse, the special wireless operator, all perished. Meanwhile, with operations against the enemy reaching a climax, it was decided by the Air Ministry to supplement the already powerful Bomber Support force by forming 171 Squadron on 7 September 1944 at North Creake within 100 Group. Initially, the Squadron, commanded by Wing Commander M. W. Renaun DFC, was formed with Stirling Mk III aircraft and crews from C Flight, 199 Squadron. No. 171 Squadron's first operation took place on 15 September, when two Stirlings took off on a special mission, which was completed successfully. Shortly after, fourteen Halifax crews were posted in from squadrons under the operational control of 4 Group HQ, but they were unable to operate as 171 Squadron's Halifaxes were held at St Athan undergoing installation of *Mandrel* and *Window* chute equipment. (Stirlings would continue to be used until 21 November.) Finally, on 21 October 171 Squadron Halifax IIIs took off on a *Windowing* operation. En route, the operation was cancelled and the aircraft recalled. However, one aircraft failed to receive the signal and pressed on to the target where it was plotted as 'a force of some thirty

Beside the former control tower is another ex-RAF building, now a private residence. Author

The Dalgety silos dwarf the wartime Nissen huts at North Creake on the B1105 Egmere to Wells-next the Sea road. Author

heavy bombers', a successful, if unintentional start for the squadron! In March 1945 199 Squadron, the last Bomber Command squadron still with Stirlings, also replaced its aircraft with the Halifax III. Both 171 and 199 Squadrons were used in the bomber-support role, using various types of countermeasures equipment including *Window* and *Mandrel*; the squadrons also flew normal bombing operations.

As the Halifaxes returned to operations in the early hours of 2/3

March 1945, intruders were in the area. Halifax III NA107/T of 171 Squadron, piloted by Squadron Leader P. C. Procter, the B Flight Commander, was attacked at 3000 feet on returning from a *Mandrel* sortie by a Ju 88. The crew of eight baled out and the aircraft crashed at Walnut Tree Farm, South Lopham. Warrant Officer A. P. Richards, the mid-upper gunner, sustained a broken ankle, while the flight engineer, Flight Sergeant H. Laking, 'apparently under the impression that there was no hope of survival and anxious to save time and money in transportation', glided into a cemetery!

The final sorties of the war from North Creake were flown on the night on 2 May 1945. At North Creake Air Vice Marshal Addy Addison was present during the take-off of thirty-eight aircraft of the Southern *Window* Force of eighteen Halifaxes from 171 Squadron and ten from 199 Squadron, also heading for Kiel on *Mandrel/Window* operations. Addison expressed his satisfaction at the size of the final effort. All told, a record 106 aircraft of 100 Group took part. Two Halifaxes from 199 Squadron, each with eight men on board and carrying four 500-lb bombs and large quantities of *Window*, probably collided while on their bomb runs. They crashed at Meimersdorf, just south of Kiel. They were the last Bomber Command aircraft to be lost on operations in World War Two. Only Pilot Officer Les H. Currell, pilot of RG375/R, who baled out

The control tower, now a house, just off the B1105 Fakenham-Wells road before the Dalgetty site. Author

with slight leg injuries, and his rear gunner, Flight Sergeant R. 'Jock' Hunter, survived. Aboard RG373/T piloted by Flight Lieutenant William E. Brooks, only Pilot Officer K. N. Crane, the rear gunner, survived. The two squadrons at North Creake had lost a total of seventeen aircraft during operations from the airfield, eight Stirling and nine Halifaxes.

No. 171 Squadron was disbanded on 27 July 1945, followed two days later by 199 Squadron. The Station Flight also disbanded in July and in late September the airfield was reduced to Care and Maintenance. Then on 13 October 1945 the station was transferred to 41 Group Maintenance Command and became No. 111 Sub-Storage Site (SSS) of 274 Maintenance Unit, which was based at Swannington. The task of 111 SSS was the long-term storage of Mosquitoes. These Mosquito aircraft were eventually taken out of storage and flown by test pilots before delivery to other units, which included the Turkish Air Force. No. 111 SSS closed in late 1948. The RAF finally relinquished North Creake in the autumn of 1947, whereupon the flying field was returned to agriculture and the runways, apart from narrow strips used as farm roads, were eventually removed. After 1948 the Ministry of Agriculture used North Creake as a grass-drying plant. Although most of the runways have been removed, hangars and smaller buildings and parts of the perimeter track survive. The former technical site buildings are used by Dalgety Agriculture's feed mill operation. The watch office is now a private residence.

CHAPTER EIGHT

OULTON

Oulton airfield, which was known locally as 'Bluestone', the name of the railway halt and level crossing adjoining the airfield, lay largely in the parish of Oulton Street to the east of the B1149 Norwich to Holt road. The site had been requisitioned early in 1940 and the landing ground consisted of a large grass field on which six Nissen huts were built. Members of the RAF Defence Force were billeted in cattle sheds at Green Farm, which were in a terrible condition. Eventually, workmen concreted the floors and installed showers and electricity. A grass landing strip was established and made ready for use by the end of July. Soon after, a number of Nissen huts were erected and by the time the first aircraft arrived about seventy personnel, including men for airfield defence, were stationed there. At first, this was just a solitary Lewis gun mounted on a pole. Later, a number of gun pits were dug around the airfield perimeter. Tall wooden poles were erected in fields surrounding the landing ground to prevent any possible landings by aircraft and gliders. For night operations a Chance light was mounted on a trailer and gooseneck flares lined the runway. All public roads around and inside the airfield boundary remained open to the public during these early days.

The airfield is in the parish of Oulton Street to the east of the B1149 Norwich to Holt road. Author

Oulton airfield opened in July 1940 as a satellite landing ground for Horsham St Faith (now Norwich Airport) controlled by 2 Group, Bomber Command. When on 9 August 1940 German bombers raided St Faith, hitting hangars and aircraft, the next day, 114 Squadron and its Blenheims were moved to the north-east Norfolk airfield. (Further attacks were made again on St Faith that evening.) The majority of the aircrews were initially housed in local dwellings and a fortunate few were billeted in Blickling Hall, now a well known National Trust property, nearby. No. 114 Squadron flew bombing operations from Oulton until March 1941, when it was sent to Thornaby for operations in support of Coastal Command. No. 2 Group then moved 18 Squadron's Blenheims to Oulton from Great Massingham in April 1941 and out to Horsham St Faith in July. No. 18 Squadron returned in November for a few weeks before returning once more to Horsham. In December, 139 Squadron appeared with Lockheed Hudsons on which the men trained before being shipped to the Far East. The Hudsons lingered on at Oulton for a while in the hands of 1428 Flight, which had been formed to provide conversion training.

No. 114 Squadron was stationed at Oulton from July 1940 until March 1941 with Blenheim IV bombers, its main targets being the Channel ports and targets in occupied Europe and Germany. On 15 December 1940, 2 Group's Blenheims took part in a major attack on Mannheim. Blenheim IV R3744 of 114 Squadron had engine failure on take-off from Oulton and jettisoned two 230-lb HE bombs on Norwich before crashing at Sprowston in Norwich. In April 1941 18 Squadron arrived with Blenheim IVs, staying until July 1941, when it was replaced by 139 Squadron, also flying Blenheims. No. 139 Squadron left in October 1941, although returning in December 1941 and June 1942. No. 18 Squadron also returned in November 1941, but left the following month.

When 139 Squadron returned to Oulton on 5 December 1941, the men trained on Hudson GR.III aircraft before being posted to the Far East, where they were to fly the type operationally for a short period before returning to the UK to fly Blenheims again with 2 Group. On 18 December 1941 Hudson III V9231 of 139 Squadron crashed on take-off from Oulton. A few days later the Squadron left for the Far East. No. 1428 Hudson Conversion Flight was formed at Oulton in late December 1941 with up to twelve Hudson GR.IIIs. On 28 January 1942 Hudson III V9098 of 1428 Flight crashed when it failed to take off at Oulton, due to icing. The Flight disbanded at Oulton on 29 May 1942. During the summer of 1942 Oulton was loaned to Coastal Command and 236 Squadron was stationed at Oulton with Beaufighter Ic aircraft from July to September

1942. The Beaus had only recently been fitted with underwing carriers for two 250-lb bombs and were in the process of conducting trials in the torpedo-bomber role against enemy shipping off the Dutch coast. The trials were so successful that 236 Squadron was transferred to North Coates to form part of the first Beaufighter Strike wing.

Typhoon Ia R7633 US-C of 56 Squadron suffered engine failure while flying in the vicinity and belly-landed on the airfield on 27 August 1942, injuring the pilot, Flight Lieutenant A. V. Gowers.

In September 1942 Prestige & Co. Ltd began work on bringing the airfield up to Class A standard. The Oulton Street to Cawston road was closed to permit the main runway close to the north-west to south-east direction (not the most common position for the main runway, but the only available site in this instance) to be extended. Two public roads going south from the village street had to be closed to enable this runway to be laid. It meant a long detour via Aylsham now for many destinations and it became almost impossible to reach the village from the south side. With the added problem of no signposts, only those who knew the area well would have found the village. The main runway was 2000 yards long and the two cross runways 1400 yards long, all runways being 50 yards wide. A concrete perimeter track with hardstandings consisting of thirty-two loop type and eleven pans linked all three runways. Three of the pans put down in earlier years on the south side near the old railway line were isolated and another four were incorporated in the new bomb dump off the north-west side. Four T2 hangars, one each side of the south-east end of the main runway, one on the Technical Site and one near Manor House at the north-west corner on the outside of the perimeter track, were erected. Two of the T2s were used for storing gliders. A completely new bomb storage site was built on the north side. Briefly, the other six sites after reconstruction included a Technical Site, with the airfield entrance situated west of the village street actually on the airfield proper. The Communal Site, which included the Airmen's Mess east of the village street, had access by a track from the street and from the sites at the back. There were also a communal and sick quarters site near Green Farm and three accommodation sites on the back road to Able Heath and Aylsham. Blickling Hall, a fine seventeenth-century mansion reputed to have associations with Anne Boleyn, was used for Officers' Quarters. In the Hall grounds were the WAAF sites and in the park nearby were the Sergeants' Mess and Quarters. Finally, opposite St Andrews Church, Blickling, was the main NAAFI building. In all, accommodation was provided for 1532 airmen and 250 WAAFs.

Fortress with H2S scanner in the nose at Oulton in 1944. via CONAM

Oulton became the satellite to Swanton Morley; 2 Group and 88 Squadron arrived from Attlebridge with Douglas Boston III bombers. On 31 October a 250-lb high-explosive bomb that had failed to release from a Boston during a sortie, exploded while being removed, killing six ground crew airmen. On Sunday 6 December 1942 the squadron took part in Operation *Oyster*, the famous 2 Group raid on the Philips works at Eindhoven. Only a few operations were possible during the winter of 1942-3 because of a shortage of Boston aircraft and on 30 March 1943 88 Squadron left for Swanton Morley. Their place at Oulton was taken on 1 April by 21 'City of Norwich' Squadron from Methwold when that station was returned to 3 Group. The men were equipped with Ventura B.I/III bombers, which were used mainly for attacking targets in occupied Europe. No. 21 Squadron left in September 1943 to convert to Mosquitoes, by which time 2 Group came under the Second Tactical Air Force. (All 2 Group's airfields in Norfolk were then transferred to 3 Group control, but Oulton never received any of 2 Group's squadrons.) During 1943 about forty Horsa gliders were stored on the airfield. The station transferred to 3 Group Bomber Command as a possible satellite to Foulsham, but the station closed while the Technical, Communal and other sites were enlarged and a control tower and at least one blister hangar and a bomb storage area were built.

Oulton reopened on 16 March 1944 under 100 Group, Bomber Command, and the new Station Commander was Group Captain T. C. Dickens. Three bomber support units arrived from Sculthorpe, which was closing for major reconstruction; 214 Squadron moved to Oulton on 16 May with Fortress B.II/III aircraft. Early in May, the American 36th Bomb Squadron (formerly the 803rd Squadron) equipped with six RCM Fortresses fitted with *Mandrel* and *Carpet* moved to Oulton. No. 1699 Flight (equipped with Fortress II/IIIs and one B.I (B-17C) aircraft) also arrived from Sculthorpe. By the end of May a total of twenty-two crews were fully converted to Fortresses.

These aircraft were used in the radar/radio countermeasures role, supporting the Main Force bombers. The RAF Fortresses had their chin turrets replaced by H₂S radar blisters and the fuselage was packed with 'black boxes'. A chute was provided in the rear fuselage for dropping *Window* and for their night role they were painted black overall and fitted with flame dampers. The American B-17s were fitted with *Mandrel* and *Carpet* jamming devices and flew mainly daylight missions.

The first loss occurred on 23/24 May 1944 when Bomber Command's main target was Aachen. One of the three RCM Fortresses despatched by 214 Squadron was SR384/A, flown by Pilot Officer Allan J. N. Hockley RAAF, which was intercepted and shot down by *Oberleutnant* Hermann Leube, *Staffelkäptain* of 4INJG3 flying a Ju 88G-I. Hockley and his mid-upper gunner Sergeant Raymond G. M. Simpson were killed; the seven other men in the crew escaped alive.

During June 1944, 100 Group began its work of deceiving the enemy, using the airborne *Mandrel* screen and *Window* feint forces. On 5/6 June, a *Mandrel* screen was formed to cover the approach of the Normandy invasion fleet and from subsequent information received, it appeared that considerable confusion was caused to the German early warning system. Four Fortresses of the 803rd (and sixteen Stirlings of 199 Squadron) established a *Mandrel* screen in a line from Littlehampton to Portland Bill. Five Fortresses of 214 Squadron flown by the CO, Desmond J. McGlinn DFC, and Squadron Leaders Bill Day and Jefferies (the A and B Flight Commanders respectively) and Flight Lieutenant Murray Peden RCAF and Flying Officer Cam Lye RNZAF, also operated in support of the D-Day operation in their *Airborne Cigar* (*ABC*) role. (*ABC* was a device consisting of six scanning receivers and three transmitters designed to cover the VHF band of the standard German R/T sets and to jam 30-33 MHz (*Ottokar*) and later 38-42 MHz (*Benito* – R/T and Beam). A protective patrol lasting over five hours was flown at 27,000 feet, starting just north and east of Dieppe and running

Liberator *M-Mother* at Oulton in 1944. via Theo Boiten

Flight Lieutenant Murray Peden RCAF (front) and Flying Officer Steve Nessner; special wireless operator, enjoying themselves on a motorcycle in front of 'Canada House' at RAF Oulton. Nessner, born in Yugoslavia of German parents, Canadian by naturalization, flew 17 trips in 100 Group in American aircraft, bombing his ancestral origins! While recovering from an ear, nose and throat operation his first crew was shot down in the circuit at Oulton on 3/4 March 1945. On 15/16 April, Nessner was injured when the Fortress he was in crash-landed in Belgium after being shot up over Schwandorf. Steve Nessner

almost perpendicular to the coastline, carrying out jamming and *Window* dropping in conjunction with twenty-four Lancasters of 101 Squadron of 1 Group. One Lancaster was shot down. Overall though, the patrol was outstandingly successful and earned a personal congratulation to all concerned by Arthur Harris, to whom he pointed out that 'the work carried out was of paramount importance in connection with the Invasion Forces'. Eric 'Phil' Phillips, the Squadron Gunnery Leader, manning the tail turret of McGlinn's Fortress, also shot down an Me 410.

On 21/22 June 1944 214 Squadron was detailed to cover an attack on the Nordstern oil plant at Gelsenkirchen. Flight Lieutenant Murray Peden, a Canadian, and his crew in *F-Fox* were attacked by a Me 410 near the target area. In the ensuing combat, the Fortress was seriously

B-24 *Ramp Rooster* of the 36th Bomb Squadron. CONAM via Stephen Hutton

damaged, the starboard inner engine was set on fire and the intercom system was put out of action. Both Flight Sergeant Alfred 'Stan' Stanley, the wireless operator, and the special operator were wounded in the attack, and Flying Officer J. B. Waters, the air bomber, gave them some timely first aid. Waters also helped to restore the intercom. A few minutes later the Fortress was attacked by a Ju 88, but coolness and good shooting on the part of Flight Sergeant Johnny Walker, the air gunner, drove off the night-fighter. Strikes were obtained on both enemy machines. With one engine still on fire, Murray Peden set course for home and, displaying great ability, successfully reached the long emergency airfield at Woodbridge, where he landed safely on two good and one partially serviceable engines. Peden, Waters and Walker were commended for their actions and Stanley was awarded the DFM for continuing to carry out his duties after being wounded. Another Fortress,

B-24 *The Uninvited* of the 36th Bomb Squadron. CONAM via Stephen Hutton

Crew of B-24 Liberator *W-William* of 223 Squadron at Oulton. L-R: Flight Sergeant Ben Buff, beam gunner; Flying Officer Joe Doolin, WOp; Sergeant Murdo McIver, beam gunner; Flight Lieutenant Gordon Bremness, pilot; Flying Officer Hal Booth, navigator; Sergeant Sam Leach, tail gunner; Sergeant Roy Storr, mid-upper gunner; Sergeant Don Prutton, flight engineer. Note the sealed Emerson nose turret painted over black and the *Window* chute protruding from the bomb bay below the flame damper under the nacelle. Don Prutton

flown by Flying Officer Johnny Cassan, failed to return from the Gelsenkirchen operation. The bomb aimer, Warrant Officer Doug Jennings, was the only survivor. He eventually returned to Oulton during August.

The 803rd Bomb Squadron left Oulton on 14 August 1944, by that time having re-equipped with B-24H and B-24J Liberators. On 23 August 223 Squadron re-formed at Oulton with Fortress B.II/IIIs and Liberator B.IVs with *Mandrel* electronic detection equipment. Although 223 Squadron was originally formed as the second *Jostle* unit, its role was set to change when in mid-July 1944 the wreckage of a German rocket, thought to be a V-2, was flown to England for scrutiny at RAF Farnborough. The missile had landed in Sweden after a test firing from the German research station at Peenemünde. Immediately, urgent steps were taken to develop a countermeasure and *Jostle* equipment was subsequently modified to the *Big Ben* configuration. However, the wreckage in the hands of the RAF Farnborough belonged not to the V-2 but the Wasserfall anti-aircraft missile, although this was not realised until after the war. In November 1944, *Big Ben* was deleted and replaced with *Carpet* and *Dina* jamming devices

By the end of August, 214 Squadron, which shared the 24-hour watch on the V-2 rocket launchings with 192 and 223 Squadrons, had completed 305 successful operational sorties as a countermeasure squadron with the loss of only three crews. It had achieved a record of no flying accidents for six months. Oulton took on a flurry of activity. By early September, 223 Squadron was up to nearly full strength. Training was begun and two American Liberator pilots helped to check out the captains. Five Liberators were allotted for this and other training. Starting on 9 September, 214 Squadron Fortresses, equipped with a special modification to the *Jostle* apparatus, had also started *Big Ben* patrols. Extensive modifications were made in the Liberators belonging to 223 Squadron and the crews were reduced by one, as the front gunners were unnecessary. A large floor space in the rear bomb cell was provided for *Window* storage and the whole of the navigator's position was enlarged and improved. Additional jammers were installed and the squadron was ready to begin *Window* patrols. On 19 September, Flight Lieutenant A. J. Carrington DFC carried out the first *Big Ben* patrol for 223 Squadron. The patrols were of four hours duration and at 20,000 feet (a new experience for many Coastal Command crews). On 23 September, Wing Commander H. H. Burnell AFC arrived to take command of 223 Squadron from Wing Commander McGlinn. The new commander continued with the training programme and operated those crews judged fit for patrol duty. Later, the squadron was left solely on this task and all crews were placed on the work. It served as a useful start for squadron crews, as these four-hour patrols entailed full briefing, de-briefing and careful maintenance of flight plans.

Very few of the groundcrew at Oulton had any experience of American aircraft, no perfect tool kits, and because of the urgency of provisioning, the Liberator aircraft were far from new. Yet, they never

Fortress III *W-William* of 214 Squadron from RAF Oulton over the Norfolk countryside. via Martin Staunton

Crew of Fortress III KJ106 BU-G of 214 Squadron who took off from Oulton at 1814 hours on 7 March 1945 for *Jostle* duties over the Hamburg area and FTR. L-R: Flying Officer N. Peters RCAF, Special Operator (KIA); Warrant Officer J. Henderson, MUG (PoW); Sergeants K. Phelan, right waist gunner (PoW); W. P. Mulhall RNZAF, flight engineer (PoW); Flying Officer G. Stewart RNZAF, pilot (KIA); Sergeant A. S. Goldson, left waist gunner (PoW); Flight Sergeants J. V. Matthews RAAF, WOp (PoW); H. L. Henderson RCAF, rear gunner (KIA); J. W. Winstone RNZAF, bomb aimer (KIA). Photo taken by the navigator Sergeant H. McClymont KIA.

lost heart and although England turned out some of its most bitter winter weather, they kept on trying and did exceptional things. Ernie Frohloff, a Canadian radar mechanic in 214 Squadron at Oulton, recalls:

Life for the ground crews was a daily routine of getting a maximum number of aircraft serviceable for the next op. Leisure time was spent at the 'large, modern NAAFI in Norwich'; 'lunches of fresh crab on the cliffside at Sheringham and Cromer', where we played golf but were warned never to try and retrieve a ball from the beach, as they were mined! After the day's work we went to our favourite pubs; the Bird in Hand opposite the main gate at Oulton; the White Hart at Marsham and the Buckinghamshire Arms adjacent to Blickling Hall, for a few quiet pints, a few games of darts, or shove-halfpenny, or just to talk. At Christmas 1944 we augmented our food parcels from home with a large goose, purchased from a local farmer and cooked by the landlady of our favourite pub in North Creake. No one instructed us in how to pluck a goose, with the result that the Radar Hut, and surrounding countryside, was white with goose feathers for weeks after!

On 16/17 September 1944, Bomber Command's operations were in support of the Allied airborne landings at Arnhem and Nijmegen in Holland. On 18 September, nine Fortresses of 214 and 223 Squadrons supplied a *Mandrel* screen off the Dutch coast and the action was repeated again at first light on the 19th. Throughout 1944 the Fortresses of 214 Squadron and the Liberators of 223 Squadron had been 'Jostling' for every major bombing raid. By December, all were of still greater assistance, being fully equipped with *Carpet* (anti-*Würzburg*) and *Piperack* (anti-SN-2), besides *Jostle* (anti-HE and anti-VHF). Mosquitoes began operating this month as jammers. Their role was a dual one. They flew to target areas on routes that took them well clear of the Main Force and on the way they made 'Y' recordings of enemy R/T traffic. Arriving at the target area, they jammed

Flight Sergeant Ron 'Jimmy' James of 214 Squadron with 'Rex' in the snow outside his Nissen hut at Oulton, January 1945. Ron James via CONAM

the enemy AI with *Piperack* and they stayed there until well after the attack was over, thus covering the withdrawal of stragglers. It was intended to increase and prolong the AI jamming in the target areas to

A wartime hut being put to good use on the old airfield site near the village pond. Author

Squadron Leader Day RCAF DFC, pilot, Pilot Officer Fitzsimmons, flight engineer and Pilot Officer Fenn, WOP at Oulton in 1944. Ron James via CONAM

which the enemy fighters would ultimately gravitate. During December, the *Mandrel* screen and *Window* Forces also kept up the good work of confusion and diversion. The Ruhr was still the favourite target, and *Window* flooding continued to be used with success. Even though 141, 169 and 239 Squadrons would not shoot down any enemy aircraft during the month, their part in the overall scheme of things was of great importance. This started on 1/2 December when a *Spoof Window* attack on the Ruhr by forty-nine aircraft of 100 Group with no losses among the eighty-one heavies that attacked Karlsrühe, Duisburg and Hallendorf, was supported by *Intruder* and high-level patrols by the *Serrate* Squadrons. They would continue this type of operation throughout the month.

No. 1699 Flight was renamed 1699 Bomber Support Conversion Unit on 24 October 1944 and added Liberators to its strength. In deteriorating weather on 15 November 1944 a 'Carpetbagger' B-24H Liberator (42-94775) of the 492nd Bomb Group (Special Operations Group) from Harrington landed at Oulton. The aircraft took off on 18 November to return to base, but a fuel cap became loose and whilst trying to land at Oulton it hit a tree and crashed, killing six of the eight crewmembers.

Joyce Palmer, a WAAF at Oulton in 1944-45, recalls her experiences at Oulton:

Being a 'townie' from the north, I was immediately struck by the beauty of Norfolk and hoped that I would still be there when the following spring came. The 'WAAFery' was situated in a clearing in a wood, probably part of the Blickling Hall Estate, just up the road from the Hall and not far from the Buckinghamshire Arms Inn. 'The Buck', as it was known, was a regular meeting place for WAAFs, airmen and aircrew and as I played the piano fairly well I was never short of a pint of wartime beer. (Have never touched a drop since!)

Many of the girls didn't get up early enough for breakfast but for those who did, it meant a cycle ride of 1½ miles to a site down a lane near Oulton village street. Having usually missed breakfast, sustenance would be obtained during a short break at 10 am at a little hut-type café opposite the main gates run by a lady of about 60 years. She always wore her hair in a bun at the back of her head. She did a roaring trade with tea and wads. Her little hut was always full of airmen and women.

Part of my duties in Signals consisted of typing the daily code sheets for the aircrew. The codes were triple-checked for accuracy, being extremely important. They were changed on a daily basis and were Top Secret. I was never told what they really meant. I heard the word *Window* mentioned many times at the section but didn't know what it was until I took the trouble to risk security and ask. They must have thought I was a good risk and told me about the thousands of strips of tinfoil, which were dropped over Germany to fool their radar systems.

After Christmas 1944 the snow came and one of the worst winters for many years descended upon the country. Many operations were cancelled because of the weather. When ops were 'off' there was a general flurry of preparation by the WAAFs for unexpected dates with their boyfriends. When ops were 'on' we girls would listen for the take-offs around 7 to 8 pm. The aircraft would leave at intervals of a few minutes and we would count them off. Then during the early morning we would count them again as they returned, having been awakened by the roar of the engines. Sometimes aircraft were missing, but we always hoped that they had engine trouble and had been diverted to other bases. On one occasion when one of the WAAFs, a lovely auburn-haired girl refused to leave her bed for several days, we thought she was ill but then we discovered that her boyfriend had failed to return. We were always wary of falling for aircrew with the sad, mostly inevitable consequences. At one stage in the war the survival rate was less than one in five.

Spring eventually arrived and my wish still to be at Oulton had been granted. I particularly remember the lovely wild flowers in the woods and along the Saxthorpe and to Aylsham roadsides, where we often went for rides on our RAF issue bikes. Other outings would be to Aylsham and to the Black Boys pub, the cinema or the 'chippy'. Sometimes we went to a field near the church to watch football or cricket matches between various RAF station teams. Sometimes we were allowed to walk in the park and grounds at Blickling Hall. Occasionally we went to Norwich, which was full of GIs complete with the almost obligatory chewing gum and jeeps. We also formed a musical concert party and performed shows on the camp and at Aylsham town hall and at Saxthorpe village for the local residents.

When it was all finally over, a grand party was held in the airmen's mess. What day (and night) VE celebrations turned out to be. Shortly after the end of the war the ground crews and WAAFs were given the opportunity of taking a trip in a bomber aircraft over to Germany to see for ourselves the damage done by our air raids. I shall never forget as long as I live the complete and utter devastation seen from the air. The cities were literally flattened and reduced to heaps of rubble. I have wondered many times since how two of the most inventive countries in the world could have wasted their best brains in five years of hammering away, destroying each other. Future generations will always ask the same questions; it was, of course, all down to one mad man. May it never happen again.

On 14 January 1945 223 Squadron lost its first aircraft when B-24 'R' piloted by Flight Lieutenant Noseworthy RCAF was hit by an enemy fighter and crashed near Antwerp. Noseworthy and one gunner had miraculous escapes but the rest of the crew was killed. On 20 February, Flying Officer J. Thompson RCAF was shot down by a night-fighter. The third Liberator to be lost was 'T', flown by Flying Officer N. S. Ayres. The only survivor was one of the special operators who escaped after the aircraft was hit and plunged into a pine forest. When this special operator recovered consciousness, which as he said, 'was a shock that nearly killed him', he found the *Jostle* equipment weighing over 600 lb lying on him. He later recovered from multiple injuries in an English

20-year old Sergeant Leslie E. Billington, engineer in Pilot Officer Bennett's crew, who was KIA in the intruder attack over Oulton on 3/4 March 1945. via CONAM

Pilot Officer H. Bennett DFC who piloted HB815/J, a 214 Squadron Fortress III Fortress, which was shot down in the circuit at Oulton by a Ju 88G flown by Leutnant Albert Döring of 10./NJG3 based at Jever on the night of 3/4 March 1945. Bennett and seven members of his crew were KIA, via CONAM

hospital. During March 1945, 223 Squadron learned that it would be converting to the Flying Fortress.

On 3/4 March 1945, when the *Luftwaffe* mounted *Unternehmen* [Operation] *Gisela*, an intruder operation over eastern England, Liberator 'B' of 223 Squadron was in the circuit at Oulton preparing to land when tracer was fired at it. Although hit, the B-24 was able to land safely. Pilot Officer H. Bennett in HB815/J, a 214 Squadron Fortress III, was about to land when he was told to go around again as his A Flight Commander, Squadron Leader Bob Davies, was approaching on three engines. As he was turning long finals and was cleared to land on runway 45, he saw Bennett climbing away and above him to his right. Then he saw a fairly long burst of cannon fire and his No. 2 engine and wing caught fire. Davies lost sight of Bennett still climbing and turning right. At this time Davies heard the tower say 'Bandits! Bandits! Switch off all lights'. All airfield lights were extinguished. Bennett and seven members of his crew were KIA. Only the two waist gunners, Sergeant Alastair McDermid and Warrant Officer R. W. Church, survived the blazing inferno. The Fortress had

97

been shot down by 27-year-old *Leutnant* Arnold Döring of 10./NJG3 from Jever.

On the night of 14/15 March 1945 when 5 Group Bomber Command attacked the Wintershall synthetic oil refinery at Lützkendorf near Leipzig, Fortresses of 214 Squadron performed *Jostle* radio countermeasure duties in support of the Main Force. HB802 piloted by Flight Lieutenant Norman Rix DFC was shot down by a Ju 88 G-6 flown by *Hauptmann* 'Tino' Becker of Stab IV./NJG6 and his radio/radar operator. Flight Lieutenant Johnny Wynne DFC, pilot of Fortress III HB799/K, flew his aircraft home alone after he had ordered his crew to bale out following a serious engine fire. He crash-landed at Bassingbourn. Five of Wynne's crew who baled out were murdered in cold blood. Between 8 February and 22 March 1945, six other 214 Squadron crews failed to return to Oulton.

No. 100 Group's presence at Oulton came to an end in late July 1945 when 1699 BSCU disbanded on 29 June and 214 and 223 Squadrons were disbanded on 27 and 29 July respectively. After the end of the war, a number of Oulton-based Fortresses were moved to RAF Foulsham to join the newly

Leutnant Arnold Döring of 10./NJG3, who with his Bordfunker (radio operator) Walter Hoyer, shot down Bennett's Fortress in the circuit at Oulton on 3/4 March 1945. Döring was a very experienced fighter pilot who had seen action during the Battles of France and Britain and in the Russian campaign. After shooting Bennett's Fortress down Döring and Hoyer destroyed a Lancaster in the sky over Lincolnshire. via Theo Boiten

The funeral of Sergeant Billington at St. Andrew's Church, Blickling. Group Captain Dickens, the Oulton station commander, is leaving the doorway. CONAM

Flight Lieutenant Johnny Wynne DFC, who brought Fortress III HB799/K back alone from Lützkendorf near Leipzig on the night of 14/15 March 1945, in the cockpit of _Take It Easy_. CONAM

formed RWE (Radio Warfare Establishment). The RWE then moved to Watton and Shepherds Grove to continue the work that had been carried out by 100 Group.

On 30 October 1945 Maintenance Command took over Oulton airfield and it became 110 Sub-Storage Site of 274 Maintenance Unit (Swannington). A large number of Mosquitoes were stored on the airfield. Later, they were taken out of storage and inspected; some were overhauled and flown out, while others were scrapped on site. No. 274

The memorial at Oulton Street. Author

MU closed in November 1947. By 1948 the RAF had departed and the road between Cawston and Oulton Street was reopened. While much of the land was reclaimed for agriculture, the runways remained and were used for locating poultry houses in isolation. In the 1950s and 1960s light aircraft and crop sprayers used the airfield. Several of the wartime buildings remain and surviving Nissen huts are used by farmers. On the north side of the airfield the old canteen is used as the village hall, while nearby is one of the old airfield defence pillboxes.

On Sunday 15 May 1994 the Bishop of Lynn formally dedicated a memorial to RAF Oulton, built of red brick at the crossroads north of Oulton Street. A total of fifty-six Bomber Command aircraft were lost flying in operations from Oulton: thirty-four Blenheims, two Bostons, a Ventura, sixteen Fortresses and three Liberators. The plaque of Cumbrian stone has the inscription, 'RAF Oulton 1940-45, in Grateful Tribute to those members of the British Commonwealth and American Air Forces who served at RAF Oulton and in honour of those that gave their lives. Those who died for our freedom will live forever in our hearts. Below is a listing of all the squadrons and units based here'. Also, a book of remembrance has been placed in St Andrew's church at Blickling.

Aerial view of Oulton airfield in June 1997 from an Army Air Corps Lynx helicopter. Author

CHAPTER NINE

SCULTHORPE

This airfield, situated between the village of the same name and Syderstone to the west, north of the A148 Fakenham to King's Lynn road, was built originally to Class A standard from 1942 to October 1943 by Bovis Ltd and Constable Hart & Co. Ltd. Construction meant closing two country roads. Three runways, the main one being 2000 yards long and the two cross runways both 1400 yards long, were laid and these were bordered by thirty-six loop hardstandings. The technical area with two T2 hangars was on the west side of the airfield, with two communal and seven domestic dispersed sites for 1773 airmen and 409 WAAFs further to the west. Two more T2s were erected on the south-east side and the north-east side. A bomb dump was built south of the technical site.

The first operational unit was 342 Lorraine Squadron, recently formed at West Raynham with French personnel. Flying Bostons, the squadron spent its first weeks at Sculthorpe continuing training and flew its first sorties on 12 June 1943, when attacks were made on a power station at Rouen. In July the French squadron moved to Great Massingham and 464 and 487 Squadrons arrived from Methwold to begin converting to Mosquito FBVIs from the Lockheed Ventura. They were soon joined by 21 Squadron, which also converted to Mosquitoes from the dreaded Ventura. All three squadrons finally joined the other 2 Group squadrons in southern England at the end of the year and 100 Group took control of Sculthorpe. The first unit was 214 Squadron from

A *Jostle* R/T jamming transmitter and its associated equipment. (IWM)

T2 hangar at Sculthorpe in April 2006. Author

3 Group at Downham Market, which at the time was equipped with Stirlings. In January 1944 214 Squadron was assisted by a small American RCM detachment (803rd Bomb Squadron) commanded by Captain George E. Paris, which arrived at Sculthorpe on 19 January to train the RAF crews in jamming using *Jostle* equipment. Early in 1944 eleven war-weary B-17Fs of the 95th, 96th and 384th Bomb Groups, 8th Air Force, arrived to join the 803rd Bomb Squadron. They were immediately fitted with *Mandrel*, *Carpet* and ELINT jamming equipment, exhaust-flame dampers for night flying and *Gee* navigation equipment. (Seven of these became drone aircraft packed with explosives and were used in Project *Aphrodite*.) *Jostle* (which began arriving in May) and *Window* patrols would form the bulk of 214 Squadron's work and for the ten months preceding the end of the war, over 1000 sorties were completed on 116 nights.

No. 214 Squadron's Stirlings gave way to Boeing Fortresses modified for electronic countermeasures with highly secret equipment. The conversion took some weeks and RCM work did not begin in earnest until April 1944 when 214 Squadron was told that it would move to Oulton as Sculthorpe was to be closed for reconstruction. New 300-foot-wide and much stronger runways replaced all the original runways, but the base was not complete until the end of the war. Post-war, Sculthorpe became a USAF base, first for temporary duty assignments by the USAF Strategic Air Command and as a permanent base until 1962. It was a stand-by base until the end of 1992 when the USAF withdrew and the base closed. The housing, mostly bungalows, built for USAF personnel and now known as Wicken Green Village, was sold in the mid-1990s.

CHAPTER TEN

SWANNINGTON

In October 1942 construction of Swannington airfield, located about 8 miles north-west of Norwich, east of the Swannington village to Brandiston road, which was closed, began after Kent & Sussex Construction Co. Ltd had received a £882,000 contract to build the base to Class A standard. The Cawston to Horsford road was also cut south of St Nicholas's church. Three concrete runways, the main at 2000 yards and two cross runways both 1400 yards long, perimeter track and thirty-six hardstandings of the loop type were constructed, as were the technical and domestic sites. Two T2 hangars were erected on the north-east of the airfield near Haveringland Hall and a B1 hangar was located just west of the bomb dump on the south side between Moegoes Plantation and Crimea Covert near Swannington village. The station was dispersed between the airfield and Hall Farm, mainly in the grounds of Haveringland Hall, which had been requisitioned for an Officers' Mess. There was one communal, one WAAF, four domestic and a sick quarters site. The airfield was not completed until early in 1944, by which time there was accommodation for 1956 airmen and 450 WAAFs.

On 4/5 November 1944 Squadron Leader Branse Burbridge DSO* DFC* and Flight Lieutenant Bill Skelton DSO* DFC* of 85 Squadron shot down three Ju 88s and this Bf 110 of II./NJG1 north of Hangelar airfield. The Messerschmitt crashed into the Rhine, killing pilot Oblt Ernst Ranze, although radar operator Obergefreiter Karl-Heinz Bendfeld and the gunner baled out safely. Burbridge and Skelton finished the war as the top scoring nightfighter team in the RAF, with 21 aircraft destroyed, 2 probables, 1 damaged and 3 VIs also destroyed. (IWM)

The station opened as part of 100 Group on 1 April 1944 and was earmarked for occupancy by two Mosquito night-fighter squadrons, 85 Squadron from West Malling and 157 Squadron from Valley. At the beginning of May 1944, 85 Squadron equipped with the American-made AI Mk X and already well trained in its use, had been engaged in defensive night-fighting, while 157 Squadron, equipped with the AI Mk XV, had supported Coastal Command's daylight anti-U-Boat patrols in the Bay of Biscay. AI Mk X, unlike Mk IV, had no backward coverage at all. From the point of view of the Mosquito's own safety, some kind of backward warning equipment had to be fitted before it could be used on high-level operations. To provide a quick interim answer BSDU began a modification of *Monica I*. Until the tail warner was fitted, 85 and 157 Squadrons would be trained for low-level airfield intrusions. This would mean that the AI Mk X squadrons would eventually be in a position to play a dual role – either high-level or low-level work, which would help considerably in the planning of bomber operations. Mosquitoes of 100 Group continued their support of the invasion forces on 6/7 June. A lack of enemy air activity in the Western Approaches had permitted the transfer of 85 and 157 Squadrons to 100 Group. These flew in to the recently completed base at Swannington. Wing Commander John Cunningham had previously commanded No. 85 Squadron and 157 Squadron had been the first unit to be equipped with the Mosquito. The squadrons were expert in the *Intruder* role. No. 85 Squadron arrived on 1 May, followed by 157 Squadron six days later. Both squadrons were to be committed to bomber support operations over enemy territory. Nos 85 and 157 Squadron officially began

85 Squadron crest.
via **CONAM**

NFXIX of 157 Squadron at its dispersal near St. Peter's Church, Haveringland on whose land part of RAF Swannington airfield was sited. Author

Mosquitoes at Swannington in 1944. Far left is Mosquito II HJ911, which had served with 157 Squadron for almost two years by the time this shot was taken and it went on to serve with 141 and 307 Squadrons and 1692 Flight before being SOC on 19 February 1945. Author

operations on D-Day, 5/6 June, when sixteen sorties were flown. Twelve Mosquitoes in 85 Squadron operated over the Normandy beachhead, while four in 157 Squadron patrolled night-fighter airfields at Deelen, Soesterberg, Eindhoven and Gilze Rijen in Holland. No. 85 Squadron despatched twelve Mosquitoes over the Normandy invasion beaches and four Mosquitoes of 157 Squadron (and ten of 515 Squadron) made *Intruder* raids on Belgian and Dutch airfields. On the night of 11 June Wing Commander Charles M. Miller DFC**, Commanding Officer of 85 Squadron, and Flying Officer Robert Symon, in a Mosquito XIX fitted with AI X, shot down a Bf 110 over Melun airfield.

The first airfield intrusion results with AI Mk X were very promising and it was found that at a height of 1500-2000 feet AI contacts at ranges of three miles or so could be obtained and held. During June, from 176 sorties despatched, of which 131 were completed, thirty-eight AI contacts were reported leading to the destruction of ten enemy aircraft and the damaging of three others. All these combats, save one of those leading to damage claims, resulted from sixty-two sorties flown between the nights of 11/12 June and 16/17 June. On 12/13 June Flight Lieutenants James Ghilles 'Ben' Benson DFC and Lewis 'Brandy' Brandon DFC opened the score at Swannington for 157 Squadron when they shot down a Junkers 188 to take Benson's personal tally to five.

Swannington airfield in June 1997. Author

157 Squadron aircrew playing snowballs at Swannington in the winter of 1944-45. via CONAM

From 25 to 27 June both squadrons left Swannington to return to West Malling for *anti-Diver* patrols since the V-1 offensive was now threatening London and southern Britain. Just over 130 successful *Intruder* patrols, out of 176 despatched, had been carried out by the two squadrons before they were transferred. They returned to Swannington on 29 August and continued to cause havoc over enemy airfields during their *Intruder* patrols. Their claims for enemy aircraft while based at Swannington with 100 Group reached seventy-one destroyed and six damaged by 85 Squadron and thirty-seven destroyed and thirteen damaged by 157 Squadron. Swannington's top night-fighter team, Squadron Leader Branse Burbridge DSO* DFC* and Flight Lieutenant Bill Skelton

The Swannington 'Hun scoreboard' showing some of 85 and 157 Squadron's victories, now on display at the City of Norwich Museum at Norwich Airport. Author

DSO* DFC*, finished their second tours early in 1945 to finish the war as the top-scoring night-fighter crew in the RAF with a final total of twenty-one victories.

The *Intruder* sorties were not without incident. On 26 September Mosquito MM648 of 85 Squadron dived into the ground at West Acre,

Swannington control tower in 2005.
Author

Norfolk, from 3000 feet, killing the crew. On 21 November 1944 MM629 of 157 Squadron was shot down by Mosquito MM630, whose pilot mistook it for a Ju 188! The crew baled out. On 15 January 1945 the crew of MV565 reported over R/T that they was having fuel problems as they were being diverted to Woodbridge owing to bad weather; nothing was ever heard of this 85 Squadron crew again. One of 157 Squadron's Mosquitoes, TA404, claimed the unusually high score of six enemy aircraft destroyed before it failed to return from a sortie on 3/4 March.

Between November 1944 and February 1945 the Spitfires of 229, 453 and 602 Squadrons were detached to Swannington from their stations at Ludham, Matlaske and Coltishall for training and special strikes – their bases were unusable because of rain and snow. The units' role at this time was patrols over the Hague area of Holland to seek V-2 launch sites, although transportation and other targets of opportunity were frequently attacked. On one such patrol, a 602 Squadron pilot, Sergeant T. L. 'Cupid' Love made a unique first, when he opened fire on a V-2 as it rose into the air in front of him. The V-2 continued, apparently undamaged. There

85 Squadron air crew at Swannington in 1945. Vaughan Collection

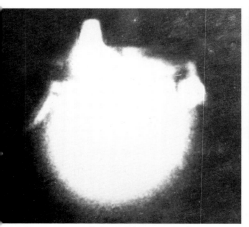

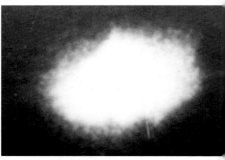

was a tragic accident on 14 February 1945 as the Spitfire XVIs of 602 Squadron were breaking to land. SM538 collided with SM353 and dived into the ground inverted, ¾ mile from the aerodrome, killing the pilot, Flight Lieutenant Lloyd. The other Spitfire managed to land at Swannington, from where the distressed pilot rushed to the scene of the crash in vain.

The Mosquitoes then flew bomber support operations right up to the end of the war, their last sorties being made on the night of 2 May 1945. During the course of operations from the station the two Mosquito squadrons lost a total of nineteen aircraft. On 27 June 1945 85 Squadron moved south to Castle Camps, while 157 disbanded on 16 August 1945. The following month 100 Group relinquished control and Swannington became the headquarters station of 274 Maintenance Unit, which received and stored surplus Mosquitoes at this and other airfields in the region.

No. 41 Group took over the station on 1 October 1945 and on this day 274 Maintenance Unit was formed with the task of storing Mosquitoes with sub-stations at Little Snoring, North Creake, Downham Market and Oulton. The Mosquitoes were flown in for storage. From late 1946 until the unit disbanded in November 1947, the aircraft were inspected, then either scrapped, used as instructional airframes or flown out by test pilots from Waterbeach to other units or air forces. Swannington airfield was kept intact until it was sold in 1957, when it reverted to agricultural use with much of the concrete broken up for hardcore. A seed-packing firm acquired the technical site, first using two hangars before erecting new units.

CHAPTER ELEVEN

SWANTON MORLEY

This airfield, two miles north-north-east of East Dereham, overlooking the south side of the Wensum valley, is unique to the region in that until the closure of RAF Swanton Morley on 6 September 1995, the station had the largest RAF grass airfield in Europe. Nine days later, on Battle of Britain Day, appropriately, the station's ensign was lowered for the last time and fifty-five years of history came to an end. In the late 1930s Swanton Morley was an expansion scheme airfield, but it was never finished to the usual standard. With war imminent, work on improving the station's overall facilities, which would cost a total of £490,000, began. Buildings were erected by Richard Costain & Co. Ltd near Mill Street on the eastern side of the airfield and several country roads, especially between the villages of Worthing and Swanton Morley, were closed. On 17 September 1940 the partly finished station – the only hangarage was a single Type J hangar that had been erected on the technical site – was opened in 2 Group Bomber Command. During the next few months tarmac hardstandings were laid around the perimeter of the grass airfield. The first unit to move to Swanton Morley was 105 Squadron, which had lost most of its Fairey Battle aircraft in the Battle of France and was in the process of receiving Blenheim IV light bombers. No. 105 Squadron moved to Horsham St Faith near Norwich on 9 December 1941 to convert to the Mosquito IV and was replaced by 226 Squadron and its Boston IIIs. No. 226 Squadron remained at Swanton Morley until 14 February 1944 when it moved to Hartford Bridge. During 1941 to 1943 four T2 hangars were erected on the airfield and thirty-one loop hardstandings and a perimeter track were laid. When work on barracks was finished, 1968 airmen and 390 WAAFs could be accommodated on the station.

On 17 December 1943 2 GSU [Group Support Unit] transferred to Fersfield in Suffolk. The Mosquito Major Servicing Section arrived from West Raynham on 31 December. Shortly after, the BSDU (Bomber Support Development Unit) workshops Section at Radlett (known as the 'Houseboat', a small but very well equipped radio laboratory and workshop to carry out the larger development and production tasks) was transferred to Swanton Morley station control and called the 'Radio

Spitfire IIA P7350 of the Battle of Britain Memorial Flight passing the Worthing side of Swanton Morley airfield during a reunion for former Arnold Scheme veterans and the Spitfire Society in 1999. Author

Engineering Section'. Moves were afoot to transfer 2 Group Headquarters in Bomber Command at Bylaugh Hall and its ten squadrons of light bombers at seven airfields in Norfolk to the 2nd Tactical Air Force, ready to support the invasion of Europe, which was planned for May-June 1944.

The BSDU arrived at Swanton Morley from Foulsham in June 1944 and was established on the Worthing side of the airfield where a T2 hangar had been erected. (The BSDU had been formed at West Raynham on 10 April 1944 under the command of Wing Commander R. F. H. Clerke DFC, initially with four Mosquitoes later increased to nine, before moving to Foulsham in June, to develop, test and produce a wide variety of radar and radio equipment for 100 Group.) In addition to the technical development and production side, a Mosquito Flight of nine aircraft was established to carry out operational and non-operational trials appertaining to fighter equipment. Among the inventions BSDU developed and introduced into service, were a range of tail warning devices; homers such as *Serrate* IV, IVA, IVB and V; *Hookah* and interrogators like *Perfectos* I, IA, IB and II. During the period June 1944 to April 1945, BSDU carried out 114 operational sorties in Mosquitoes over the continent to test the various fighter devices.

The crews who flew these operations were experienced 100 Group pilots and navigators. Among their ranks were Flight Lieutenant Donald 'Podge' Howard DFC and Flight Lieutenant Frank A. W. 'Sticky' Clay DFC. 'Sticky' Clay recalls:

The night-fighter crews who completed a first tour in 100 Group could expect to go for their first 'rest' of six months. They went either to BSTU (Bomber Support Training Unit), or to BSDU, with the noticeable difference that they would still be expected to carry on operating because the new equipment could only be adequately tested operationally. My time was enjoyable. I lived with my wife and infant son in rooms in East Dereham. Living-out, I got as a Flight Lieutenant 18/2d a day pay (non-flying). The married allowance was 7/6d a day and about 3/6d a day ration allowance, something like 2/- a day lighting and heating allowance and 11/- a day batting allowance. I think we paid the lady in Swanton Morley £3 a week for the three of us – full board! There were many parties and Saturday evenings in the mess. We had a splendid little band, led by LAC Ray Ellington, quite a jazz star. (We used to leave our baby son in a basket in a WAAF Officer's bedroom.)

The nature of our operations was such that we (more or less) planned our own trips after seeing the morning Bomber Command Broadcast, which gave details of the targets for the night. It was nice too to try out various 'boxes' dreamed up by George Baillie (one of the boffins), and then use them operationally. I remember him sitting on a chair on the perimeter track with earphones on, listening to pulses emanating from a sort of Wall's Ice Cream tricycle being ridden around the other side of the airfield by some poor 'erk'. [George Baillie was one of the small group of scientists who pioneered electronic warfare at the Royal Aircraft Establishment, Farnborough, in the late 1930s. Inspired by Group Captain 'Addy' Addison, Baillie's team anticipated that the *Luftwaffe* would use radio beams to guide bombers to targets in Britain. As a result of their dedicated efforts in the run-up to the outbreak of war, the RAF was amply prepared for the 'Battle of the Beams', and in 1940 radar started to be introduced in night-fighters. At the height of the Battle of Britain Baillie was posted to Radlett, Herts, where Addison had formed Bomber Command's 80 Wing to counter enemy beams. Equipment was scarce, but Baillie employed all the ingenuity for which the cash-starved Farnborough scientists were renowned to turn hospital radiotherapy sets into beam-benders. After America's entry into the war Baillie paid regular visits to the United States to pass on Britain's growing expertise in electronic warfare. His overall contribution to the development of Britain's radar capabilities played a significant part in the eventual success of 100 (Bomber Support) Group.]

On the night of 13/14 February 1945 when the bombers' targets were Dresden and Leipzig, Howard and Clay were airborne in their Mosquito XIX and they returned having destroyed a Bf 110. On the night of 19/20 April 1945 they flew another successful BSDU sortie from Swanton Morley when they destroyed a Ju 88. In all, BSDU crews scored five air-to-air victories.

Date	Aircraft	Details	Crew
6/7.12.44	Mosquito XIX MM638 'G'	Bf 110 W of Giessen	S/L N. E. Reeves DSO DFC* F/O M. Phillips
13/14.2.45	Mosquito XIX MM684 'H'	2 x Bf 110 Frankfurt area	F/L D. R. Howard DFC F/L F. A. W. Clay DFC
4/5.4.45	Mosquito XXX NT540 'C'	Bf 109 W Magdeburg	S/L R. G. Woodman DFC F/L A. J. Neville DFC
19/20.4.45	Mosquito XXX NT276 'B'	Ju 88 S Denmark	F/L D. R. Howard DFC F/L F. A. W. Clay DFC

Flight Lieutenant H. E. 'Harry' White DFC* and his navigator/radio-operator, Flight Lieutenant Mike Seamer Allen DFC* were posted to BSDU on 14 June 1944. (On 28/29 July 1944 this crew returned briefly to West Raynham to fly *Serrate* patrols with nine other Mosquitoes of 141 Squadron. During the sortie they shot down two Ju 88s to bring their tally to twelve, the highest score in the Squadron's history. Their total was increased by one in the post-war years when Martin Middlebrook's research for his book *The Peenemünde Raid* revealed that a Bf 110 claimed only as 'damaged' on 17/18 August 1943, had actually been destroyed.) White and Allen flew twenty-one and twenty operations

Harry White and Mike Allen of 141 Squadron, one of 100 Group's most successful pairings with 12 enemy aircraft destroyed and three damaged.

Their final claim was for a Ju 88 damaged whilst flying an NFXXX with the BSDU in January 1945.
(Mike Allen)

respectively while with the BSDU, testing new radar equipment for 100 Group. In August, for example, they tested the gyro fixed gunsight as fitted to a Mosquito XIX of the Fighter Interception Unit at Wittering. In September, both men received a second Bar to their DFCs.

White and Allen had a narrow escape on 2/3 January 1944 after take-off from Swanton Morley in Mosquito NFXXX MM797, an aircraft that was something of a jinx on the unit as it caused them repeated problems during operational flights in late 1944. On 12 November 1944 for instance, White and Allen took off in MM797 for an operation to Essen in the Ruhr. They were halfway down the runway when the port engine failed. White hauled back on the starboard throttle and eventually brought the Mosquito to a stop on the grass extension to the runway a few yards short of the fence. Again, the ground crew, when they had towed MM797 ignominiously back to the dispersal bay, could find nothing wrong with the engine. By the end of the year MM797 was known throughout BSDU as the 'dreaded XXX'.

On 2/3 January 1945 White and Allen took off in MM797 in support of a raid by the Main Force on the Ruhr. It was their ninety-first operation. When glycol started pouring out of the port engine shortly after taking off, White pressed the feathering button and jettisoned the long-range drop tanks. He was at 600 feet, too low to think of turning to get back into Swanton Morley and too low for either of them to bale out.

113

Herbert Farrow, Harry White and Mike Allen. Mike Allen

When he found the propeller of the dead engine would not fully feather, he knew he could not maintain height for very long. He realised his only chance was a belly landing into a field, if he could spot one in the gathering darkness. Harry White skilfully got the Mosquito down on the frozen ground more or less in one piece, but both men were trapped in the wreckage. Fortunately, Herbert Farrow, a farmer, and James Andrews, one of his labourers, who were working on Broadway Farm at Scarning, and Walter William Ward, known as 'Old Walter', had seen the Mosquito crash. Old Walter was at work in the woods nearby at the time of the crash. Farrow, Andrews and Old Walter raced to the scene and saw that one of the airmen in the cockpit was unable to get out because his leg was trapped. At the risk of their own lives, they succeeded in pulling the airmen out with the flames growing in intensity and explosions of ammunition. A second or two after all five men flattened themselves in a ditch nearby, the petrol ignited and the Mosquito exploded. The two RAF men owed their lives to these three men. By 14 January, White and Allen were operational again. When his left leg had thawed out Mike Allen went to goldsmiths and silversmiths in Regent Street in London

Harry White and Mike Allen of the BSDU had a narrow escape on 2/3 January 1944 after taking off from Swanton Morley in Mosquito NFXXX MM797 in support of a raid by the Main Force on the Ruhr. Glycol started pouring out of the port engine shortly after taking off and White had to skillfully put the aircraft down in a field. Three locals rescued the trapped airmen. Mike Allen

and ordered three silver tankards, suitably inscribed, which they presented to their rescuers at a party at Broadway Farm attended by some of their old friends from 141 Squadron and the villagers of Scarning. On 8 May 1945 Farrow, Andrews and Old Walter were awarded the BEM (British Empire Medal). It was bitter for Mike Allen to learn from Herbert Farrow that, after the war was over, he and Walter Ward and Jimmy Andrews were sent their BEMs through the post! However, Herbert did not seem to be too troubled by that. What he really seemed to value was his silver tankard!

After VE-Day the *Window* Research Station, which had been in existence for several months at Swanton Morley, was transferred to the BSDU. With the disbandment of 100 Group in the summer of 1945, Swanton Morley lay largely dormant until December 1946 when 4 Radio School (later 1 Air Signallers, then Air Electronic School) with Proctors, Prentices and Ansons was established at the airfield and remained until late 1957. Swanton Morley continued in operation for ground units until its closure on 6 September 1995, the only flying being carried out by gliders for the ATC. A flying club and a microlight school on the Worthing side of the airfield closed in 1996 when the airfield was taken over by the British Army for Robertson Barracks. The J and T2 hangars were demolished for new AFV buildings, but the rare watch office with meteorological section designed in 1939 was saved.

CHAPTER TWELVE

WEST RAYNHAM

This station, 5 miles south-west of Fakenham and 2 miles west of West Raynham village, began life as a grass airfield during 1938-9 and opened on 5 April 1939 with four Type C hangars and brick buildings north-west of the landing ground. Construction caused the Coxford to Kipton Ash road to be closed to the public. No. 2 Group took over the station and Blenheims of 101 and 90 Squadrons moved here from Bicester in May 1939. During 1940-41, thirty-six pan-type standings were built. No. 2 Group continued to use the station and other units also took up residence at various times until the spring of 1943 when its resident squadron and 1482 (B) G Flight moved out, the latter to Great Massingham. The station then closed and the boundaries to the west were extended to accommodate two new hard runways, one 2000 yards in length and one 1400 yards, and perimeter track. The runways were completed by November 1943. During the construction programme by Allot Ltd, fourteen loop-type standings were added to take the final number to thirty-seven and increased accommodation could now cater for 2456 airmen and 658 WAAFs.

The wartime control tower. Author

141 SQUADRON RANGER EFFORT

BAGGED *(commencing: 19·7·4...)* BY 141 SQUADRO...

141 Squadron Ranger Effort scoreboard which was taken out of store at RAF Quedgley, Glos, and put on display in one of the hangars at West Raynham on 1 June 1994 for the closure ceremony. Author

'Bagged by 141 Squadron' scoreboard. Author

No. 100 Group took over the station on 3 December 1943 when the Group HQ was established on the station on a temporary basis until the permanent HQ at Bylaugh Hall near Swanton Morley was ready for occupation on 18 January 1944. West Raynham was the new home for 141 Squadron, the first operational squadron in 100 Group, and conversion from Beaufighter IVfs to Mosquito IIs began in earnest. No. 239 Squadron joined 141 Squadron at West Raynham and both squadrons Mosquitoes were fitted with *Serrate* to home in on airborne radar carried by *Luftwaffe* night-fighters. No. 239 Squadron had been training at Ayr and Drem since September 1943 for *Serrate* Bomber Support operations. On 11 December 1943 two operational Mosquito IIs equipped with AI Mk IV forward-looking and backward-looking *Serrate* equipment and the *Gee* navigational aid arrived. The squadron trained at every available opportunity when the weather allowed. For twelve nights from 4 December, not one heavy bomber had operated because of a full moon and bad weather. When Bomber Command resumed operations on

239 Squadron seated and standing in front of one of their Mosquitoes at West Raynham in late spring 1944. Wing Commander Paul Evans, the CO, is seated fifth from left, front row.
Tappin Coll

16/17 December with a heavy attack on Berlin, two Beaufighters and two Mosquitoes of 141 Squadron took off from West Raynham on 100 Group's first offensive night-fighter patrols in support of the heavies. It was hardly an auspicious occasion and became known as 'Black Thursday'. Bomber Command lost twenty-five Lancasters and a further thirty-four Lancs were lost on their return to England due to very bad weather causing collisions, crashes and some bale-outs after aircraft ran out of fuel.

On 20/21 December a raid on Frankfurt resulted in forty-one bombers being lost. No. 141 Squadron despatched two Beaufighters, one of which returned almost immediately because of intercom trouble. On 23/24 December the target was Berlin. No. 141 Squadron put up three Beaufighters for the night's operation. One Beaufighter was forced to abort when the *Serrate* equipment became inoperative and a second crew was never seen again. The third Beaufighter, flown by Flight Lieutenant Howard Kelsey DFC and Edward Smith DFM, returned triumphant, having scored 100 Group's first victory, a Ju 88 near Duren.

NF.XXX of 239 Squadron flown by Warrant Officer Graham 'Chalky' White over Hamburg at the end of the war just after hostilities had ended. Graham White

NFIIs first equipped 157 Squadron on 13 December 1941. DD750, which served with 157, 25, 239 and 264 Squadrons, is fitted with AI Mk.IV 'arrowhead' and wing mounted azimuth aerials. All four machine guns were deleted to make room for *Serrate* apparatus. The all-black scheme could slow the aircraft by up to 23 mph. via Philip Birtles

On 5/6 January, when Bomber Command raided Stettin, 141 Squadron mounted its last Beaufighter *Serrate* sortie of the war. Unfortunately, the war weary Mosquito IIs were found to be lacking in performance and problems with AI radar and *Serrate* took time to be rectified. (From February to March 1944 the Mosquitoes were re-engined with Merlin 22s and in the second half of 1944 they were supplemented by some FBIVs.) Meanwhile, on 27/28 January when a force of 515 bombers attacked Berlin, losses were high again: thirty-three Lancasters were shot down. No. 141 Squadron despatched seven *Serrate* Mosquitoes and 239 and 169 Squadrons sent off three and two Mosquitoes respectively However, none of the Mosquitoes recorded any successes, mainly because five crews experienced engine failures and had to abort, while two other aircraft suffered AI failures. On 28/29 January seven Mosquitoes were despatched from West Raynham. One returned early with equipment failures and Flight Lieutenant Basil 'Johnny' Brachi and his navigator, Flying Officer Angus P. MacLeod of 239 Squadron, failed to return. Flying officer Harry White DFC and Flying officer Mike Allen DFC of 141 Squadron destroyed a Bf 109 and Flying Officers Munro and Hurley of 239 Squadron scored the first Squadron victory using *Serrate*, with a Bf 110 destroyed near Berlin. White and Allen became legendary in 141 Squadron, destroying a further eight night-fighters in the air while stationed at West Raynham from February to July 1944, taking their tally to thirteen in all, the highest score in the Squadron's history. In total, during the period February 1944 to April 1945, 141 Squadron Mosquito night-fighter crews destroyed thirty aircraft in the air and 239 Squadron, fifty-eight aircraft.

Flight Lieutenant (later Squadron Leader DFC and 'A' Flight Commander) Geoffrey E. Poulton and Flying Officer (later Flight Lieutenant DFC) Arthur J. Neville of 239 Squadron, who destroyed a Ju 88G-1 and damaged another near Eindhoven on 17/18 June 1944. via Ron Mackay

On 8/9 June 1944 Flying Officer A. C. Gallacher DFC and Warrant Officer G. McLean DFC of 141 Squadron destroyed an unidentified enemy aircraft over Northern France after they had chased it into a flak barrage at Rennes, where it was brought down by a single burst. A popular Free French crew, Flight Lieutenant D'Hautecourt and his navigator Pilot Officer C. E. Kocher, returned from their seventh operation, patrolling over their homeland, on one engine and belly-landed DD758 at West Raynham only to wing off the runway and crash into two Spitfires. Both Frenchmen, who had only been with the Squadron since February, and another airman, were killed.

Flying Officer Taffy Bellis DFC* of 239 Squadron scored six air-to-

Flight Sergeant Frank H. Baker, navigator-radar operator and his pilot Flying Officer (2nd Lieutenant) R. D. S. 'Hank' Gregor, USAAF of 141 Squadron. On 14/15 March 1945 'Hank the Yank and Frank' were on a lone ASH patrol in the Frankfurt-Mannheim area in support of the bombers attacking Zweibrücken near Saarbrücken, when they shot down a UEA coming into land at Lachen airfield. The enemy aircraft exploded under their nose just as they began pulling out after closing rapidly to 100 ft. The explosion illuminated the area, and almost at once they drew light flak and were coned by a searchlight, which Gregor dodged by turning into it and diving. This victory was 141 Squadron's final air-to-air kill of the war. Molly Baker Collection

air victories flying Mosquitoes from West Raynham from 31 May to 8/9 August 1944 with his pilot, Flight Lieutenant Denis Welfare DFC*. He recalled that they were lucky to be in the squadron at the right time, 'with fine aircraft and equipment and, most of all, to be part of the happiest squadron imaginable'.

Another factor was West Raynham itself – it was a pre-1939 station with all the comforts that implied. Important too was the fact that most of the aircrews were flying Mosquitoes for the first time – it was an aeroplane that crews had a lifetime love affair with. In fact, our wives and sweethearts complained that they had to share our affections with the Mosquitoes! Lastly, there were the personnel themselves. Types such as the tolerant CO Paul Evans, the flight commanders, the irrepressible 'Jackson' Booth and 'Golden' Neville Reeves and his navigator 'Mad' Mike O'Leary. Adj Hawley always had a ready smile and nothing was too much trouble for him. Then there was 'Buster' Reynolds – Buster was the Chief Intelligence Officer. He was a solicitor in civvy life and not only was he a thorough and relentless debriefer of crew returning from ops, but also he was the drinking and singing leader during the never-to-be-forgotten mess parties.

In December 1944 239 Squadron converted to Mosquito NFXXX night-fighters. The same month the Mosquitoes of 141 Squadron were fitted with ASH centimetric radar and *Monica*, a tail warning device. No. 239 Squadron returned to operations in January 1945, flying high- and low-level patrols. In March 1945 141 Squadron also converted to Mosquito NFXXXs, becoming operational in April when seven of its aircraft dropped napalm bombs on Neubiberg airfield. It became the first RAF squadron to use this weapon.

On 6, 12 and 13 April 1944 Wing Commander 'Winnie' Winn DFC, the CO of 141 Squadron, carried out trials of types of napalm gel when he dropped 100-gallon drop tanks on the grass at West Raynham. Napalm gel is petrol thickened with a compound made from aluminium, naphthenic and palmitic acids hence 'napalm' – to which white phosphorous is added for ignition. It came in three different consistencies – thick, medium and thin. The trials caused enormous interest and the station and aircrew crowded in the control tower while the groundcrews climbed onto the roofs of the hangars in order to get a better view of the explosions. It was decided that crews who would drop napalm gel required no additional training because they had carried out enough low-level attacks with bombs or cannon over many months; no special tactics were to be employed. Enthusiasm and keenness to get on the night's napalm gel programme reached a fever pitch. When six aircraft were asked for, a dozen were offered – and accepted! Petrol and range were reduced so that each Mosquito could carry two 100-gallon drop tanks of napalm gel but, even so, they would have to land at Juvincourt, Melsbroek or Mannheim.

The first napalm gel or *Firebash* raid went ahead on 14/15 April when Potsdam near Berlin was attacked. Eighteen Mosquito VIs and XXXs (twelve from 141 Squadron and six from 239 Squadron) were despatched from West Raynham. Seven Mosquitoes of 141 Squadron flew high-level AI Mk X patrols in support of the Potsdam raid, but also covered the remaining five 141 Mosquitoes. They were to carry out the first napalmgel *Firebash* raid on night-fighter airfields at Neuruppin near Potsdam (three napalm-carrying Mosquitoes) and Jüterborg near Berlin (two napalm-carrying Mosquitoes). At Neuruppin all six drop tanks containing fifty gallons of napalm gel exploded near the hangars and engulfed the airfield in flames and smoke. At Jüterbog the two crews

West Raynham closure ceremony on 1 June 1994. Author

tossed their napalm bombs on the estimated position of the airfield (one drop tank hung up). All five fire-bomber Mosquitoes landed back at Melsbroek for refuelling before returning to West Raynham.

The second *Firebash* raid by 141 Squadron was flown on 17/18 April when two out of five Mosquitoes sent to attack Schleissheim airfield just north of München were successful in appalling weather conditions. The squadron's third *Firebash* raid took place on the night following, 18/19 April 1945, when seven Mosquitoes, each carrying two 100-gallon drop tanks filled with napalm, were despatched to München/Neubiberg airfield. On 19/20 April 141 Squadron dropped napalm on Flensburg airfield on the Danish border. Further napalm gel attacks were carried out on 22/23 April when Jägel was attacked by Mosquito XXXs of 141 Squadron (and three Mosquitoes of 169 Squadron and four Mosquitoes of 515 Squadron). A 141 Squadron Mosquito flown by Flight Lieutenant G. M. Barrowman and Warrant Officer H. S. Griffiths suffered severe damage in the starboard wing and inner fuel tank. They returned to England hugging the German and Dutch coasts, keeping the Friesians in sight to port, and landed safely at Woodbridge. On 23 April, as part of the support operation for the ground troops, five Mosquitoes of 23 Squadron flew to Melsbroek with six napalm Mosquitoes of 141 Squadron led by Wing Commander Winnie Winn, refuelled and crossed to Lübeck. That night, they

A deserted West Raynham in the summer of 1994. Author

One of the 239 Squadron scoreboards which was taken out of store at RAF Quedgeley, Gloucestershire and put on display in one of the hangars at West Raynham on 1 June 1994 for the closure ceremony. Where are these scoreboards kept, now that RAF Quedgeley has closed? Author

plastered the airfield with HE, incendiaries and fire bombs under the direction of Master Bomber Squadron Leader D. I. Griffiths of 23 Squadron. The whole attack took just ten minutes; the airfield was left burning and devastated. All aircraft returned safely despite light, accurate flak put up by the defenders. On 24/25 April six Mosquitoes of 141 Squadron carried out a napalm attack on München/Neubiberg airfield again. Squadron Leader Harry White DFC** and Flight Lieutenant Mike Allen DFC** claimed the destruction of a single-engined enemy aircraft on the ground – the last recorded victory for 141 Squadron in World War Two.

The last operation was on 2 May 1945 when eight Mosquito XXXs of 239 Squadron took off from West Raynham for high-level and low-level raids on airfields in Denmark and Germany. Six Mosquitoes of 141 Squadron made napalm attacks on Flensburg airfield with fourteen napalm-armed Mosquitoes attacking Hohn airfield.

No. 141 Squadron moved to Little Snoring on 3 July 1945 and on the last day of the month 239 Squadron disbanded. Bomber Command operations carried out from this station during the war claimed eighty-six aircraft: fifty-six Blenheims, twenty-nine Mosquitoes and a Beaufighter. RAF West Raynham was transferred to 12 Group Fighter Command and a succession of famous operational units and squadrons operated from the station until July 1991. The last unit to be based here was 66 Squadron, equipped with Rapier missiles until the summer of 1991. The station closed on 1 June 1994.

SUMMARY OF THE AIRFIELDS & OTHER LOCATIONS

BLICKLING HALL

Blickling, Norwich NR11 6NF (tel: 01263 733084, fax: 01263 734924).

Description: Billet for 2 Group and 100 Group personnel in World War Two.

Location: 1 mile west of Aylsham on B1354 Aylsham to Saxthorpe road signposted off the A140 Cromer Road.

Directions: If visiting Oulton, carry on through the village past the memorial to the first T-junction and turn right. Travel along the B1354 Aylsham to Saxthorpe road. From Aylsham, head along the B1354 towards Saxthorpe. Blickling Hall is on the right.

Comments: Whether you are an aviation enthusiast or not, no visit to Norfolk is complete without a visit to one of the greatest houses in East Anglia. On a fine day a walk around the lake, which was once used by RAF airmen in simulated dinghy drills, set in the 4,777-acre estate, is well worth completing. The Hall also looks particularly impressive at night. Apart from an RAF museum in the outbuildings of the hall, other highlights include a spectacular Jacobean plaster ceiling in the long gallery; eighteenth and

Map of the Blickling estate. Author

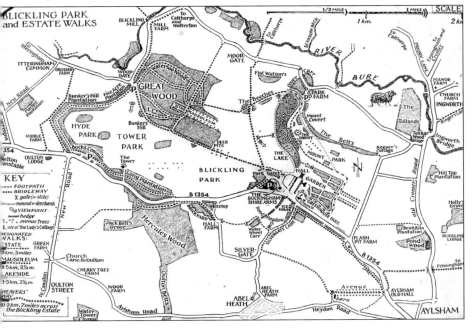

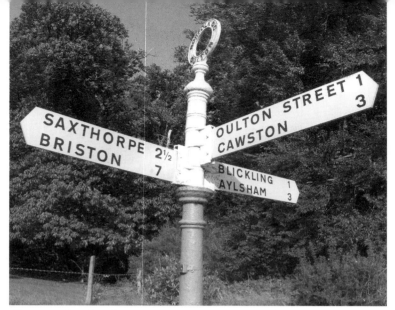

Signpost showing Oulton airfield's proximity to Blickling Hall. Author

nineteenth century furniture collections; a distinguished library of 12,000 books; a tapestry of Tsar Peter the Great; a formal woodland wilderness garden with daffodils, bluebells, azaleas and rhododendrons; a secret garden with summerhouse and scented plants; Victorian parterre garden with herbaceous borders; mature yew hedges and topiary; woodland walks/plant sales; a shop; and a restaurant and a tea-room with children's menu. Finally, if the lakeside walk and a day spent touring airfields is too much, then the Buckinghamshire Arms immediately next to the Hall offers hotel accommodation, a bar and four-poster-bedded rooms!

Opening Times: House: 4 April to end of July – Wednesday to Sunday and bank holiday Monday 1-4.30 pm; September to November Wednesday to Sunday 1-4.30 pm. Last admission 4.30 pm. Garden: same days as house 10.30 am to 5.30 pm (gates close at 6 pm) and open daily 1-30 August, 2 November to 31 March. Sundays only 11am to -4 pm. Park and woods: open daily all year dawn to dusk. Lunches and teas in restaurant: 4 April to 1 November when house and garden are open 10.30 am 5.30 pm; 2 November to 20 December, Thursday to Sunday 10.30 am to 5.30 pm.

BYLAUGH HALL

Description: HQ for 2 Group and 100 Group in World War Two.
Location: Off the B1147 road towards Lyng and Elsing, near Swanton Morley airfield.

Directions: On minor road off the B1147 heading for Lyny. Hall is on the hill on the left.

Comments: Well worth a look during your visit to Swanton Morley and the surrounding area. The Hall, which spent many years in a derelict conditon with the roof missing, has now been fully restored to its former glory. Nearby are a few Nissen huts.

CITY OF NORWICH AVIATION MUSEUM (CONAM)
Old Norwich Road, Horsham St Faith, Norwich NR10 3JF (tel: 01603 893080).

Description: Aviation museum featuring the 100 Group Memorial Room and historical aircraft and exhibits.

Location: On the northern edge of Norwich International Airport (formerly RAF Horsham St Faith), which offers a good view of the passenger aircraft flying from this expanding regional airport.

Directions: Leaving Norwich, take the A140 towards Cromer and turn right off the bypass after the main airport entrance.

Comments: No trip to the region's airfields and tourist attractions is complete without rounding everything off or starting with a visit to this museum, which was conceived and is run by a dedicated band of

The 100 Group Stafford Sinclair Memorial Room at the City of Norwich Aviation Museum at Norwich Airport. Author

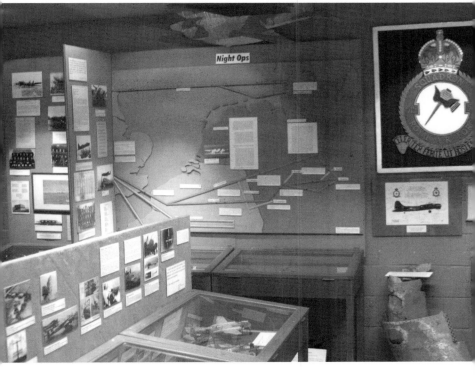

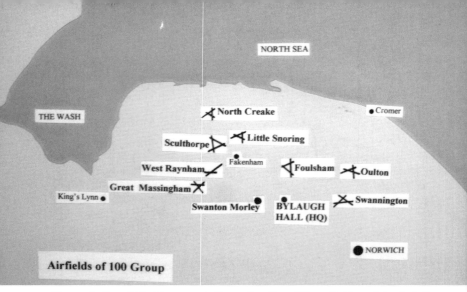

NORTH SEA

THE WASH

North Creake

Cromer

Little Snoring

Sculthorpe

Fakenham

West Raynham

Foulsham

Oulton

Great Massingham

King's Lynn

Swanton Morley

BYLAUGH
HALL (HQ)

Swannington

NORWICH

Airfields of 100 Group

Map of the 100 Group stations in the City of Norwich Aviation
Museum. Author

The 100 Group Stafford Sinclair Memorial Room at the City of
Norwich Aviation Museum. Author

A model of a 223 Squadron Liberator and a mascot, which was carried on operations, in the 100 Group Stafford Sinclair Memorial Room. Author

volunteers. A Vulcan bomber dominates the Museum's collection and a variety of other aircraft, both civilian and military, are also on display. Within the Museum's exhibition building are displays showing the development of aviation in Norfolk. Pride of place has to go to the Stafford Sinclair Room, which is dedicated to the operations of 100 Group, the centrepiece of which is the superb black scoreboard of kills by 85 and 157 Squadrons, which once adorned a wall at Swannington. An excellent gift shop sells books, models and other items. Opening times: April to October – Tuesday to Saturday 10.00 am to 5.00 pm. Sunday and bank holidays: 1200-5.00 pm. School holidays: 1200-5.00 pm. November to March: Wednesday and Saturday 10.00 am 4.00 pm. Sunday and bank holidays: 12.00-4.00 pm. Closed over Christmas and New Year. Admission prices vary. Children under 5 free.

FOULSHAM
Description: Light bomber, heavy bomber and 100 Group airfield in World War Two.
Location: 15 miles north-west of Norwich in the parishes of Wood Norton and Foulsham and a half mile north of Foulsham village.

Directions: Follow the A1067 Norwich to Fakenham road and turn right just after the water tower to your left. Drive on through Foulsham village, stopping to inspect the village sign with its reference to the local airfield, and head towards Hindolveston, taking great care on the winding, twisting road. The airfield buildings that remain are on your left.

Comments: Three hangars remain intact at Foulsham and in between them are several buildings, either disused or in use by local industry. Above the doorway of one of the buildings are the painted letters 'Ground Equipment'.

Unit	From	To	Aircraft	Sqdn Code
192 Sqdn	Oct 1943	Feb 1944	Halifax II/III/V; Mosquito IV/PRXVI; Anson I; Wellington X	DT
1473 Flight	Dec 1943	Feb 1944	Wellington III; Anson I	
BSDU	May 1944	20.12.44	Mosquito FBVI/NFXIX	
7th Photo Group	Aug 1944	Mar 1945	P-38J (F-5) Lightning USAAF	
171 Sqdn	Sept 1944	Oct 1944	Stirling III; Halifax III	6Y
462 RAAF Sqdn	Dec 1944	Sept 1945	Halifax III	Z5
199 Squadron	July 1945	June 1946	Halifax III	EX

GREAT MASSINGHAM

Description: Light bomber, day bomber and 100 Group night intruder airfield in World War Two.

Location: 2 miles from West Raynham on a site directly adjacent to Great Massingham village.

Directions: Great Massingham can be reached via the Bawdeswell to King's Lynn (B1145) road, branching off right just after crossing the A1065 Swaffham to Fakenham Road.

Comments: Great Massingham is a picturesque village with a large pond and delightful little shops. Now a private airfield, it is easily accessible as part of the perimeter track is a public footpath, but apart from the runways only a single T2 hangar remains. On the western side of the village there is a water tower and a well-preserved RAF gymnasium. The Fox and Pheasant and Royal Oak, popular wartime pubs in Great Massingham, are now private residences. Weasenham Hall nearby, was requisitoned by the RAF to billet the aircrews at the end of

1940 following a heavy German bombing raid on 27 October, after which it was decided that aircrew accommodation should be dispersed.

Leave the village and head for the A148 Fakenham to King's Lynn road, make an immediate turn left to Little Massingham's St Mary's church and the seven RAF graves in the graveyard. Airmen who served at Great Massingham included Pilot Officer (later Squadron Leader) Bill Edrich, the England cricketer, Flight Sergeant Kenneth Wolstenholme, the famous post-war football commentator, and Keith Miller, the Australian all-rounder. Wolstenholme's New Zealand navigator, Sergeant John C. 'Polly' Weston, is one of the airmen buried in St Mary's churchyard. Returning to the main road, turn left and a few hundred yards further on to the left back from the road is Little Massingham Manor, now a convent and the religious retreat that in World War Two was used as an officers' mess by RAF units at Great Massingham.

Unit	From	To	Aircraft	Sqdn Code
1694 Bomber Def Training Flight	Apr 1944	Jul 1945	Martinet TT.1	
169 Sqdn	Jun 1944	Aug 1945	Mosquito FBVI/NFXIX	VI
1692 Bomber Support Training Unit	Jun 1944	Aug 1945	Mosquito FBVI/NFXIX/TIII; Beaufighter Vf; Wellington XVIII; Anson I; Oxford II	
CFE	Oct 1944	Aug 1945	Mosquito; Spitfires; Tempest II	

LITTLE SNORING

Description: No. 3 Group night bomber and 100 Group night intruder airfield in World War Two.

Location: North of the A148 Fakenham to Holt Road and east of the Little to Great Snoring road.

Directions: Take the A1067 Norwich to Fakenham road, branching off right just after the turn to Great Ryburgh. This avoids having to skirt Fakenham and will bring you out on the busy A148 Fakenham to Holt Road. Turn right and take the second turning to Little Snoring. The airfield is to your right.

Comments: The airfield is still in use and the control tower situated in the middle of the airfield remains relatively intact. Make a point of visiting St Andrew's church near the airfield where the 23 and 515 Squadron

Wing Commander 'Sticky' Murphy DSO DFC (left, centre) and Group Captain Bertie Rex O'Bryen 'Sammy' Hoare DSO DFC* (right centre) at Little Snoring where Murphy commanded 23 Squadron and Hoare was Station Commander. (Tom Cushing Coll)

victory boards are to be found. Outside the church is a memorial stone inscribed 'Lucy N. Hoare, died 22.6.70 aged 49, WAAF Section Officer, RAF Little Snoring 1945 and Group Captain B. R. O. Hoare DSO & Bar, Officer Commanding Little Snoring 1944-45. Died 26.3.47'. This stone was dedicated during a reunion of 23 and 515 Squadrons in 1991. In April 1944 Group Captain B. R. 'Sammy' O'Brien Hoare DSO DFC*, Commanding Officer of 605 Squadron, assumed the post of Station Commander at Little Snoring. Despite losing an eye before the war when a duck shattered the windscreen of his aircraft, Sammy Hoare became one of the foremost *Intruder* pilots in the RAF. He had commanded 23 Squadron from March to

Little Snoring with St Andrew's church in the distance. Author

The village sign. Author

September 1942 and on 6 July had flown the Squadron's first Mosquito *Intruder* sortie. In September 1943 he had assumed command of 605 Squadron, destroying a Do 217 on his first operation, and in January 1944 had notched the Squadron's 100th victory when he downed a Ju 188. At Snoring, 23 and 515 Squadron crews took bets on which one of Sammy's eyes, one blue, one brown, was real. Sammy's main feature was his moustache, which was six inches, 'wing tip to wing tip'.

The village sign in The Street at Snoring includes a propeller and Mosquito aircraft. Almost opposite the sign is the White House Guest House run by Bryan and Celia Lee (01328 878789), which is an ideal location to break your journey. Many ex-100 Group veterans and their families stay here.

Unit	From	To	Aircraft	Sqdn Code
169 Sqdn	Dec 1943	Jun 1944	Beaufighter VI; Mosquito II	VI
1692 Flight	Dec 1943	Jun 1944	Defiant I; Beaufighter II; Anson I; Oxford II; Mosquito FBVI	
515 Sqdn	Dec 1943	Jun 1945	Blenheim V; Beaufighter If; Mosquito II/FBVI	3P
USAAF *Intruder* Detachment	Mar 144	Apr 1944	P-51 Mustang; P-38 Lightning	
23 Sqdn	Jun 1944	Sept 1945	Mosquito FBVI/NFXXX	YP
141 Sqdn	Jul 1945	Sept 1945	Mosquito NFXXX	TW
No. 2 CAACU	Jun 1950	Apr 1953	Spitfire XVI; Mosquito TT35; Vampire FBV	

NORTH CREAKE

Description: 100 Group RCM bomber airfield in World War Two.

Location: 5 miles north-west of Fakenham and 2 miles east of North Creake village.

Directions: Although the airfield went under the name of North Creake, it is nowhere near the village of the same name on the B1355. It can best be reached by travelling along the B1105 Egmere to Wells-next-the-Sea road, which passes straight past the airfield with buildings and silos immediately to your left.

Comments: Of particular interest is the watch office, which is to the left before the Dalgety Agriculture feed mill operational site silos behind a tree-lined bend. It has been converted to a private residence and should therefore be treated with respect and courtesy before photographing. One of the T2 hangars survives. The North Creake operations board is now on permanent display at the Norfolk and Suffolk Aviation Museum

The Dalgety site at North Creake airfield. Author

Nissens by the side of the road at North Creake airfield. Author

Massive silos towering over Nissens at North Creake airfield. Author

The wall painting of Stirling III LJ531 EX-N of 199 Squadron, which was carefully extracted by the Fenland Aircraft Preservation Society in 1983 and put on permanent display in the RAF Bomber Command Museum at Hendon. Author

at Flixton, near Bungay, Suffolk.

In 1983 a mural depicting Stirling III LJ531 EX-N of 199 Squadron, which was painted on a brick wall of one of the airfield buildings, was carefully extracted by the Fenland Aircraft Preservation Society and put on permanent display in the RAF Bomber Command Museum at Hendon. Underneath the mural is the inscription 'Chop 16-6-44 R.I.P.', which refers to the fact that on the night of 16/17 June 1944 this aircraft disappeared in the North Sea with Pilot Officer T. W. Dale RNZAF and his six crew and Flight Sergeant F. Lofthouse, the special wireless operator, during a *Mandrel* screen operation. Actually, a front view of the Stirling was painted on one wall and on the reverse of the same wall was the back view of the aircraft; only the facing view of the aircraft is shown at Hendon.

Unit	From	To	Aircraft	Sqdn Code
199 Sqdn	May 1944	Jul 1945	Stirling III; Halifax III	EX
171 Sqdn	Oct 1944	Jul 1945	Stirling III; Halifax III	6Y

OULTON

Description: Light bomber, heavy bomber conversion and 100 Group RCM airfield in World War Two.

Location: In the parish of Oulton Street to the east of the B1149 Norwich to Holt road.

Directions: Take the B1149 Norwich to Holt road and the next turn right after the roundabout on the Cawston to Aylsham road (B1145). Be very careful after taking the right turn to Oulton Street when driving because nearing the end of the airfield runway (huts will be seen on your left) a semi-concealed hump in the road is liable to take your undercarriage off!

Comments: A few huts remain, the control tower being demolished in December 1999 after being declared unsafe. Combine your visit with a stop at the memorial at the far end of the village, before proceeding to Blickling Hall. The National Trust house and park with its lake will delight the whole family and the Buckinghamshire Arms has a bar and accommodation, including four-poster beds. A walk around the lake and fishing is free. Do not forget to seek out the RAF memorabilia in the Hall (which entails a mountaineering-style trek up to the old servant's quarters in the Gods), or the adjacent St Andrew's church where Sergeant Billington is buried.

Unit	From	To	Aircraft	Sqdn Code
1699 Flight	May 1944	Jun 1944	Fortress I/II/III (B-17E/F/G); Liberator VI (B-24H)	
214 Sqdn	May 1944	Jul 1945	Fortress IIa/III	BU
803rd Bomb Sqdn/ 36th Bomb Group USAAF	May 1944	Aug 1944	B-17F/G; B-24H/J/M Liberator	
223 Sqdn	Aug 1944	Jul 1945	Fortress II/III; Liberator IV	6G
274 MU	Nov 1945	Nov 1946	Mosquito (storage)	

SCULTHORPE

Description: Light bomber and RCM training airfield for 100 Group in World War Two.

Location: Between the village of Sculthorpe and Syderstone to the west, north of the A148 Fakenham to King's Lynn road.

Directions: Take the A148 Fakenham bypass towards King's Lynn and turn right onto the A1067 Docking road.

Comments: Extremely difficult to view as the air base is part of STANTA and is used by MoD and USAAF units, mainly by Army Air Corps and RAF units on exercise in the region.

Unit	From	To	Aircraft	Sqdn Code
214 Sqdn	Jan 1944	May 1944	Fortress II (B-17F)	BU
803rd Bomb Squadron USAAF	Mar 1944	May 1944	B-17F/G	

SWANNINGTON

Description: Primarily, 100 Group night *Intruder* airfield in World War Two.

Location: About 8 miles north-west of Norwich, east of the Swannington village to Brandiston road.

Directions: Head along the A19067 Norwich to Fakenham road and turn right towards Haveringland or along the B1149 and turn left towards Haveringland.

Comments: The watch tower, albeit 'modified' for industrial use, and parts of the technical site remain. St Peter's church, Haveringland, on whose land part of RAF Swannington airfield was sited, still looks an imposing building in the middle of the airfield. A framed photo of a wartime 157 Squadron Mosquito beside the church can be found in the Rat Catchers pub at the Cawston crossroads. The grave of Flying Officer Jeffrey N. Edwards, a navigator in 157 Squadron, is in the churchyard at the rear of St Peters. Edwards and his pilot, Flight Lieutenant William Taylor, were killed on 22/23 December 1944 when they crashed in NFXIX TA392 while attempting to make an approach to land at Swannington after informing Flying Control over the R/T that they had

The grave of Flying Offi Jeffrey N. Edwards, a navigator in 157 Squad at St. Peter's church, Haveringland. Author

St. Peter's church, Haveringland on whose land part of RAF Swannington airfield was sited. Author

157 Squadron gathered on the steps of the Officers' Mess (Haveringland Hall) at Swannington. The hall is now no more.
Richard Doleman via Theo Boiten

no aileron control. That same month the crew had scored a hat-trick of victories; on 2/3 December, a Ju 88 at Osnabrück; on 4/5 December a Bf 110 at Limburg and on 18/19 December an He 219 He 219A-O in the Osnabrück area.

Haveringland Hall, which was used as the Officers' Mess, was demolished after the war. The Swannington 'Hun scoreboard' showing some of 85 and 157 Squadron's victories, which was once stored at a caravan site at Haverlingland, is now on display at the City of Norwich Museum at Norwich Airport.

Unit	From	To	Aircraft	Sqdn Code
157 Sqdn	May 1944	Aug1945	Mosquito NFII/XIX/XXX	RS
85 Sqdn	May 1944	June 1945	Mosquito XIII/XVII	VY
229 Sqdn	Nov 1944	Dec 1944	Spitfire XVIe	
451 Sqdn	Feb 1945	Apr 1945	Spitfire XVI	

SWANTON MORLEY

Description: Light bomber, day bomber and 100 Group support airfield in World War Two.

Location: 2 miles north-north-east of East Dereham, the 100 Group facility on the Worthing side of the grass airfield.

Directions: Follow the A47 Norwich to King's Lynn road and turn off where the sign says Swanton Morley Windmill. Head on through the village and turn left towards the base, although unless you are in the Army or have prior permission, entry is out of the question. You would be better served driving on to Worthing and visiting the more accessible side of the airfield.

Comments: Now known as Robertson Barracks, the J and T2 hangars were demolished for new AFV buildings prior to Army occupation, but the rare watch office with meteorological section designed in 1939 was saved. The base is normally inaccessible to the general public for obvious reasons, but the T2 hangar on the Worthing side of the airfield can be reached by following the road through the village and turning sharp left before the church and along a rough winding road past a pillbox.

Unit	From	To	Aircraft	Sqdn Code
BSDU	21.12.44	May 1945	Mosquito FBVI/NFXIX	
100 Group Mosquito Servicing Section	31.12.44	May 1945		
Window Research Section	Feb 1945	May 1945		

WEST RAYNHAM

Description: Day light bomber, night *Intruder* and 100 Group night *Intruder* airfield in World War Two.

Location: 5 miles south-west of Fakenham and 2 miles west of West Raynham village.

Directions: Take the A1067 Norwich to Fakenham road and branch off left along the B1145 to a point where it meets the A1065. Turn right and follow signs for West Raynham (not forgetting to see Great Massingham during the journey).

Comments: Much to see, including the Station HQ, chapel, Airmen's Restaurant (with upstairs cinema) and hangars etc., as the station remains relatively intact, although in a state of disrepair following its closure in 1994.

Unit	From	To	Aircraft	Sqdn Code
141 Sqdn	Dec 1943	Jul 1945	Mosquito II/FBVI/NFXXX	TW
239 Squadron	Dec 1943	Jul 1945	Mosquito II/FBVI/NFXXX	HB
BSDU	10.4.44	May 1944	Mosquito FBVI/NFXIX	

ELY CATHEDRAL, CAMBRIDGESHIRE

In the north choir aisle is the Royal Air Force window dedicated to 2, 3, 6 and 100 Groups, which flew from airfields in the surrounding countryside.

100 GROUP
ORDER OF BATTLE

Sqdn	Aircraft	1st Op in 100 Group	Base
192	Mosquito BIV/BXVI/ Wellington BIII, Halifax III/V Mosquito II	December 1943	Foulsham
141	Beaufighter VI Mosquito II/VI/XXX	December 1943	West Raynham
239	Mosquito II/VI/XXX	20 January 1944	West Raynham
515	Mosquito II/VI	3 March 1944	Little Snoring Great Massingham
169	Mosquito II/VI/XIX	20 January 1944	Little Snoring Great Massingham
214	Fortress II/III	20/21 April 1944	Sculthorpe/Oulton
199	Stirling III/ Halifax III	1 May 1944	North Creake
157	Mosquito XIX/XXX	May 1944	Swannington
85	Mosquito XII/XVII	5/6 June 1944	Swannington
23	Mosquito VI	5/6 July 1944	Little Snoring
223	Liberator VI/ Fortress II/III	cSept 1944	Oulton
171	Stirling II/Halifax III	15 Sept 1944	North Creake
462 (RAAF)	Halifax III	13 March 1945	Foulsham

Associated Units: 1692 BSTU (formerly 1692 Flight); 1694 Flight; 1699 Flight; Bomber Support Development Unit and The *Window* Research Section.

BIBLIOGRAPHY

Baldwin, Jim (editor) RAF Sculthorpe: *50 Years of Watching & Waiting* (Privately published) 1999

Bartram, Len *RAF Docking & Bircham Newton* (Privately published)

Bartram, Len *RAF Foulsham 1942-54* (Privately published)

Bartram, Len *RAF Langham 1940-58* (Privately published)

Bartram, Len *RAF Matlaske 1940-45* (Privately published)

Bartram, Len *RAF North Creake 1940-47* (Privately published)

Bartram, Len & Hambling, Merv, *RAF Oulton 1940-47 A Brief History* (Privately published)

Bowman, Martin W. & Cushing, Tom *Confounding the Reich: The RAF's Secret War of Electronic Countermeasures in WWII* (Pen & Sword Aviation) 2004

Bowman, Martin W. *Fields of Little America* (Wensum Books, PSL, GMS) 1977

Bowman, Martin W. *The Men Who Flew The Mosquito* (Pen & Sword Aviation) 2003

Bowman, Martin W. *Mosquitopanik!* (Pen & Sword Aviation) 2004

Bowman, Martin W. *Echoes of East Anglia* (Halsgrove Publishing Ltd) 2006

Bowman, Martin W. *Low Level From Swanton* (ARP) 1995

Bowyer, Michael J. F. *Action Stations 1: East Anglia* (PSL) 1990

Confound and Destroy RAF 100 Group Association newsletters

Congdon, Philip *Behind the Hangar Doors* (Sonik)

Fairhead, Huby *Decoy Sites* (Norfolk & Suffolk Aviation Museum)

Fairhead, Huby & Tuffen, Roy *Airfields & Airstrips of Norfolk & Suffolk* (Norfolk & Suffolk Aviation Museum)

Francis, Paul *Military Airfield Architecture From Airships to the Jet Age* (PSL) 1996

Freeman, Roger *Airfields of the Eighth Then and Now* (After the Battle) 1978

Freeman, Roger *Bases of Bomber Command Then and Now* (After the Battle) 2001

Freeman, Roger *The Mighty Eighth in Colour* (Arms & Armour) 1991

Freeman, Roger *The Royal Air Force of World War Two in Colour* (Arms & Armour) 1993

Greenslade, Ron *'Signals Wallah at Large'* (unpublished)

Gunn, Peter B. *RAF Great Massingham: A Norfolk Airfield at War 1940-1946* (Privately published) 1990

Gunston, Bill *Aircraft of World War 2* (St Michael) 1981

Hilling, John B. *Strike Hard – A Bomber Airfield at War* (Sutton) 1995

Innes, Graham Buchan *British Airfield Buildings of the Second World War* (Midland) 1995

Innes, Graham Buchan *British Airfield Buildings Expansion & inter-War Periods* (Midland) 2000

Jefford, Wing Commander C. J. *RAF Squadrons* (Airlife Publishing Ltd) 1988

Marriott, Leo *British Military Airfields Then & Now* (Ian Allan Publishing) 1997

Moyes, Philip *Bomber Squadrons of the RAF and their Aircraft* McKenzie, Roderick *Ghost Fields of Norfolk* (Larks Press) 2004

Narborough Airfield Research Group *The Great Government Aerodrome* (Privately published) 2000

Peden, Murray, *A Thousand Shall Fall*

Smith, Graham *Norfolk Airfields in the Second World War* (Countryside) 1994

Streetley Martin, *Confound and Destroy*

Streetley Martin, *The Aircraft of 100 Group*

Walker, Peter M. *Norfolk Military Airfields* (Privately published) 1997